DRINK, DRUGS
AND DRIVING

AUSTRALIA
The Law Book Company Ltd.
Sydney : Melbourne : Brisbane

CANADA AND U.S.A.
The Carswell Company Ltd.
Toronto

INDIA
N. M. Tripathi Private Ltd.
Bombay

ISRAEL
Steimatzky's Agency Ltd.
Jerusalem : Tel Aviv : Haifa

MALAYSIA – SINGAPORE – BRUNEI
Malayan Law Journal
Singapore

NEW ZEALAND
Sweet & Maxwell (N.Z.) Ltd.
Wellington

PAKISTAN
Pakistan Law House
Karachi

DRINK, DRUGS AND DRIVING

BY

H. J. WALLS, B.Sc., Ph.D.

Formerly Director of the Metropolitan Police
Forensic Science Laboratory

AND

ALISTAIR R. BROWNLIE, M.A., LL.B.

Solicitor Supreme Courts
Edinburgh

LONDON
SWEET & MAXWELL

EDINBURGH
W. GREEN & SON

1970

Published in 1970 by
Sweet & Maxwell Limited of
11 New Fetter Lane, London
and W. Green & Son Limited
of St. Giles Street, Edinburgh
Printed in Great Britain by
Northumberland Press Limited
Gateshead

S.B.N. Paperback 421 14800 4

PREFACE

THERE have, during the past few decades, been many changes in the law relating to drink and driving. However, the Road Safety Act 1967 has for the first time brought British law in this field into line with that of several other countries and in so doing has introduced a new offence—that of driving whilst having more than a prescribed level of alcohol in the blood, regardless of the effect which this may have on the driver.

The Act rests on a large but not always easily accessible body of scientific data, and its implementation has required the use of new highly sophisticated analytical techniques. Lawyers and others concerned with drink-and-driving cases may well, therefore, especially if their experience in the field is limited, feel bewildered or oppressed by a sensation of being lost in a scientific jungle. This book is an attempt to provide a short and comprehensible guide to the paths through that jungle.

The Act of 1967 did not repeal the provisions of the Road Traffic Acts of 1960 and 1962 relating to driving whilst being under the influence of drink or drugs and we have, therefore, included information relevant to this offence.

The book necessarily falls into two sections—a legal and a scientific. In the legal section, we have dealt both with the definitions and concepts inherent in the law on the subject, and with the statutory and case law—both English and Scottish—as it stands at the present time (that is, up to the end of September 1969). The scientific section includes: the brief facts about alcoholic drinks; a discussion (as non-technical as possible) of the absorption and elimination of alcohol in the body; a résumé of what is known of the effects of alcohol, with particular reference to driving; some discussion of the various practical problems associated with securing blood and urine specimens; and an explanation for the non-scientist of the analytical techniques used.

Since our main text was completed a number of appeals have been decided arising from the Road Safety Act 1967. Of these it is only necessary for us to draw attention to two—*D.P.P.* v. *Carey* (1969) 113 S.J. 962 in which it was finally made clear that the instructions which accompany the Alcotest device, though not forming part of the strict law, are to be dealt with by the police in the light of common sense, and *R.* v. *Jones* (1969) 113 S.J. 963 in which the Court of Appeal approved the conviction of a motorist pursued by police from the roadway into his private garden where they administered a breath test. This liberal reading of the Act would however only cover a case in which the actions of following and testing the accused could be regarded as part of a single continuous transaction.

Where proper names appear in the text in italic type, they indicate the authorities cited by us. The full citations appear in Appendices 1 and 2 so that the reader may, should he wish, obtain more information than it has been possible to include in a book of this size, on any matter which is of particular interest to him.

H. J. WALLS
ALISTAIR R. BROWNLIE

ACKNOWLEDGMENTS

THE authors are particularly grateful to Dr. Charles H. Johnson for his authoritative help in connection with those sections of the book which deal with the work of the police surgeon or other examining doctor. They would also like to express their gratitude to: Professor R. Bonnichsen (Stockholm) for permission to reproduce figures 4 and 8; Professor R. F. Borkenstein (Indiana University) for permission to reproduce figure 10; Professor J. P. Payne (Royal College of Surgeons) for much helpful advice on medical matters and for permission to reproduce figures 6 and 7; Dr. R. L. Williams (Director, Metropolitan Police Laboratory) for his help and co-operation and for permission to reproduce figure 12; Mr. R. I. Savage (Laboratory of the Government Chemist) for information about alcoholic drinks and the time spent in imparting it; Mr. David Neylan (Metropolitan Police Laboratory) for much helpful criticism of several chapters; the Directors of most of the Forensic Science Laboratories in England, Scotland and Northern Ireland for information about drug cases.

CONTENTS

TABLE OF CASES

Lawrie *v.* Stevenson, 1968 S.L.T. 342 158
Leach *v.* Evans (1952) 116 J.P. 410; [1952] 2 All E.R. 264 124
Leck *v.* Epsom Rural D.C. [1922] 1 K.B. 383; 91 L.J. K.B. 321; 126 L.T. 528; 86 J.P. 56; 38 T.L.R. 275; 66 S.J. 439; 20 L.G.R. 173 . 137
Lockhart *v.* Coakley, 1969 S.L.T. (Sh. Ct.) 26 139

MacDonald *v.* Bain, 1954 S.L.T. (Sh. Ct.) 30; 1954 70 Sh. Ct. Rep. 61 124
— *v.* Carmichael, 1941 S.L.T. 81; 1941 J.C. 27; 1940 S.N. 83 . . 119
— *v.* Crawford, 1952 S.L.T. (Sh. Ct.) 92; 1952 68 Sh. Ct. Rep. 244 . 124
— *v.* Kubirdas, 1955 S.L.T. (Sh. Ct.) 50 124
— *v.* MacDonald (1955) 71 Sh. Ct. Rep. 17 124
— *v.* McEwan, 1953 S.L.T. (Sh. Ct.) 26; 1953 69 Sh. Ct. Rep. 47 . 121
McKay *v.* MacLeod, unreported 136
MacLean *v.* Hall 1962 S.L.T. (Sh. Ct.) 30; 1962 77 Sh. Ct. Rep 161 120
— *v.* McCabe, 1964 S.L.T. (Sh. Ct.) 39 119
MacLeod *v.* Baxter (Edinburgh Sheriff Court, May 16, 1969) Unreported 153
— *v.* Milligan; Farrel *v.* Coakley (1969) 14 J.L.S. 253 135
— *v.* Nicol, 1964 J.C. 4 157
— *v.* Parker (Edinburgh Sheriff Court, November 25, 1968), Unreported 143
MacNeill *v.* Dunbar, 1965 S.L.T. (Notes) 79 121
— *v.* Fletcher, 1966 J.C. 18 158
McNicol *v.* Peters, 1969 S.L.T. 261 . . . . 133, 138
Miller *v.* Howe [1969] 1 W.L.R. 1510; 113 S.J. 706; [1969] 3 All E.R. 451; [1969] Crim. L.R. 491 139
Moore *v.* Wilkinson [1969] Crim. L.R. 493 143
Morton *v.* Confer [1963] 1 W.L.R. 763; 127 J.P. 433; 107 S.J. 417; [1963] 2 All E.R. 765; 61 L.G.R. 461 123
— *v.* Young (Stranraer Sheriff Court, May 21, 1969), Unreported . 133
Muir *v.* Sutherland, 1940 J.C. 66 154
Murray *v.* Muir, 1950 S.L.T. 41; 1949 J.C. 127 125

Neish *v.* Stevenson, 1969 S.L.T. 229 122
Newberry *v.* Simmonds [1961] 2 Q.B. 345; [1961] 2 W.L.R. 675; 125 J.P. 409; 105 S.J. 324; [1961] 2 All E.R. 318; 59 L.G.R. 309 120
Northfield *v.* Pinder [1969] 2 W.L.R. 50; 112 S.J. 884; [1968] 3 All E.R. 854; [1969] Crim. L.R. 92 . . . . 124, 157

Paterson *v.* Ogilvy, 1957 S.L.T. 354; 1957 J.C. 42 121
Pinner *v.* Everett [1969] 1 W.L.R. 1266; [1969] 3 All E.R. 257; [1969] 119 New L.J. 438; [1969] Crim. L.R. 378 . . . . 133, 134
Punshon *v.* Rose (1968) 113 S.J. 39; *The Times*, December 12, 1968 153
Purves *v.* Muir, 1948 S.L.T. 529; 1948 J.C. 122 121
Purvis *v.* Hogg (1969) 113 S.J. 388; [1969] Crim. L.R. 378 . . . 134

R. *v.* Agnew (1968) 113 S.J. 58; [1969] Crim. L.R. 152 153
— *v.* Arnold [1964] Crim. L.R. 664 120
— *v.* Brush [1968] 1 W.L.R. 1740; 13 2 J.P. 579; 112 S.J. 806; [1968] 3 All E.R. 467; [1968] Crim. L.R. 619 140
— *v.* Burdon (1927) 20 Cr. App. R. 80 . . . . 112, 125
— *v.* Carr (1934) 24 Cr. App. R. 199 113
— *v.* Chapman [1969] 2 W.L.R. 1004; 133 J.P. 405; 113 S.J. 299; [1969] 2 All E.R. 321; [1969] Crim. L.R. 269 . . . . 135-137, 139
— *v.* Clarke [1969] 1 W.L.R. 1109; [1969] 2 All E.R. 1008; 113 S.J. 428; [1969] Crim. L.R. 441 . . . . 133, 137
— v. Clarke [1969] 2 W.L.R. 505; 133 J.P. 282; 113 S.J. 109; [1969] 1 All E.R. 924 139
— *v.* Collinson (1931) 23 Cr. App. R. 49 121
— *v.* Cook [1964] Crim. L.R. 56; *The Times*, October 30, 1963 . 122
— *v.* Davies (No. 2) [1962] 1 W.L.R. 1111; 126 J.P. 455; 106 S.J. 393; [1962] 3 All E.R. 97; 46 Cr. App. R. 292 . . . . 128, 155

TABLE OF STATUTES

CHAPTER 1

INTRODUCTION

ALCOHOL AS DRUNK

Note: This introductory chapter deals solely with the factual background information about alcoholic liquors which is desirable for a complete discussion of drinking and its effects. Any reader who finds it oppressively technical can skip it without prejudice to his understanding of the succeeding chapters, and return to it later for such information as he requires.

To chemists the word "alcohol" means a member of a class of carbon compounds possessing a certain structural feature in common and having therefore certain predictable chemical properties. The structural feature is the presence in the molecule of one or more *hydroxyl* groups each attached to a carbon atom. (Hydroxyl is one oxygen and one hydrogen atom linked together, and written in chemical formulae as—OH.) This carbon atom (or atoms, if there is more than one hydroxyl group) is in turn part of a molecular skeleton having a certain specified structure.

Alcohols were formerly named by prefixing to the word "alcohol" the name of the carbon-atom skeleton to which the hydroxyl was attached: methyl alcohol, ethyl alcohol, propyl alcohol, etc.* In the now accepted nomenclature, however, alcohols are named by giving the suffix "-ol" to the accepted name of the parent carbon compound: thus, methanol, derived from methane; ethanol; propanol, etc.†

Thus a very large number, probably thousands, of alcohols are

---

* The "-yl" ending of these words is pronounced "-ile," not "-il." In particular, ethyl is pronounced "eethile," with a marked stress on the first syllable, and not as "Ethel."

† The ending "-ol" also appears in the names of many *phenols*—another class of compounds also containing hydroxyl groups but attached to a different type of carbon-atom skeleton. No confusion need however arise here, as we shall have no further occasion to mention phenols.

known to chemists. Compounds as diverse as methanol (wood alcohol, wood spirit), ethylene glycol (used in anti-freeze), glycerol (glycerine), menthol and cholesterol are all alcohols. However, one member of the class is so overwhelmingly the most important, best known and most exhaustively studied that it is commonly without ambiguity referred to simply as "alcohol" (and will be so referred to here)—that is, ethyl alcohol, or ethanol, the compound in which a hydroxyl group is attached to a skeleton of two carbon atoms which otherwise contains only hydrogen. Its structural formula written in full is therefore

$$\begin{array}{ccc} & H & H \\ & | & | \\ H - & C - & C - OH \\ & | & | \\ & H & H \end{array}$$

but chemists always use the briefer (and entirely unambiguous) notation C_2H_5OH.

Ethanol is the alcohol present in, and responsible for the effect of, fermented or distilled potable liquors. Pharmacologically, it is therefore mankind's oldest and most widely used drug; we shall return to that aspect of its properties. In its pure state, it is a colourless mobile liquid, with a sharp taste and a characteristic smell, miscible with water in all proportions, boiling at 78° C, having a specific gravity of 0·793, and burning when ignited with a lambent colourless flame.

The alcohol in all potable liquors is derived from the fermenting of a sugar by a yeast of the genus *Saccharomyces*. There is however a limit to the alcoholic strength of any liquor made by simple fermentation, in that yeasts cannot live in the presence of more than a certain concentration of alcohol, and fermentation therefore ceases when this concentration has been reached. The precise limit depends upon the species and strain of the yeast, but it lies very roughly somewhere around 15 per cent. of alcohol by volume.

Alcoholic liquors may therefore be divided into: (1) those made by fermentation only—namely, beers, cider and table wines; (2) those in which the alcohol concentration is increased by distillation —namely spirits and liqueurs; (3) "fortified" wines—that is, liquors such as port, sherry and madeira, which are fermented wines strengthened alcoholically beyond the possible limit of fermentation by the addition of a distilled spirit, usually brandy.

The concentration of alcohol by distillation is made possible by the fact, already mentioned, that its boiling-point is lower than that of water. When a mixture of alcohol and water is heated to boiling, the greater volatility of the alcohol means that the vapour—and hence the condensed vapour, the distillate—contains relatively more alcohol than the original liquid. It is not however possible to separate alcohol and water completely by simple distillation; the purest alcohol that can be produced in this way still contains about $4\frac{1}{2}$ per cent. of water, and is usually known as *rectified spirit*. Other steps are necessary to prepare pure, or *absolute*, alcohol.

The most important fact about any potable liquor, from the points of view both of its effect upon the drinker and of the excise duty chargeable upon it, is the amount of alcohol it contains. This may be expressed in various ways. It is however ambiguous to refer simply to a percentage of alcohol present, without qualification, because of the different specific gravities of alcohol and water. As water is the substance to which all specific gravities are referred, its specific gravity is by definition 1·0, and 100 millilitres of water therefore weigh 100 grams. The specific gravity of a dilute solution of alcohol will also be not far from 1·0 and 100 millilitres of it will also weigh approximately 100 grams. Do then 100 grams, or millilitres, of a "1 per cent." solution of alcohol contain 1 gram (1·26 millilitres) or 1 millilitre (0·793 gram) of alcohol? More concentrated solutions of alcohol will of course have themselves a specific gravity significantly less than one, and unqualified definition becomes even more ambiguous. A further complication arises from the fact that the admixture of alcohol and water produces a diminution in the gross volume; if one volume of alcohol and one volume of water are mixed, the mixture will occupy less than two volumes.

A "percentage" in this context will therefore have a definite meaning only if certain qualifying information is also given. Take for example a "10 per cent." solution. This may mean:

10% weight/weight (w/w): 10 grams of alcohol in 100 grams of solution

10% volume/volume (v/v): 10 millilitres of alcohol in 100 millilitres of solution

10% weight/volume (w/v): 10 grams of alcohol in 100 millilitres of solution

10% volume/weight (v/w): 10 millilitres of alcohol in 100 grams of solution.

The last of these is never used in practice, but any of the first three may be.

If the concentration of a solution of alcohol is given as such-and-such a per cent. "by weight" or "by volume", these can be taken as meaning weight/weight and volume/volume, respectively. With comparatively dilute solutions, the specific gravity of which does not differ significantly from 1.0, the weight/weight and weight/volume percentages will be practically the same; this will not be the case however with concentrated solutions such as distilled spirits.

In scientific contexts, the concentrations of alcohol solutions are always expressed in one of the above ways, or an equivalent, but for historical reasons in both this country and the U.S.A. the tax charged on potable liquors is based on their alcoholic strength expressed in terms of a hypothetical *proof spirit*. To most people not professionally concerned with the subject, this archaic system causes considerable confusion, which is not lessened by the fact that the official proof spirits of this country and of the U.S.A. differ in their alcoholic contents.

British proof spirit was first given statutory definition by the Spirits (Strength Ascertainment) Act 1818, but it is currently defined by the Customs and Excise Act 1952, s. 172. This Act, whilst explicitly repealing earlier legislation, gives a definition which is, except for certain details of wording, identical with that given in 1818. According to it, proof spirit is a solution of alcohol in water of such a strength that at 51° F it has a specific gravity $^{12}/_{13}$ (0·92308) that of water at the same temperature; at 20° C its specific gravity, measured against that of water at the same temperature, is 0·91702, and it contains 49·276 per cent. of ethyl alcohol by weight or 57·155 per cent. of ethyl alcohol by volume.

The official proof spirit of the U.S.A. is defined as a solution of alcohol containing 50 per cent. volume/volume at 60° F. This contains, it will be seen, less alcohol than British proof spirit. In fact, "100 proof" (U.S.A.) is equivalent to 87·4 proof (British), and "100 proof" (British) is equivalent to 114·3 proof (U.S.A.).

The alcoholic strength of a liquor when quoted in terms of proof spirit is a figure which signifies the number of volumes of proof spirit that could be obtained from 100 volumes of the liquor. Thus, a liquor of strength "30 proof" would contain in 100 volumes enough alcohol to make 30 volumes of proof spirit. This figure would normally be quoted in practice as "30 degrees proof," or "30

		British Proof Strength	% Alcohol v/v	Approximate weight of alcohol per drink	
				Grams	Measure
Beer	Draught Bitter	4½-8	2½-4½	11½-20	Pint
	Draught Mild	4½-5	2½-3	11½-13½	Pint
	Bottled (Light Ales, etc.)	4½-7	2½-4	6-9	
	Bottled ("Export" & other strong Light Ales)	ca. 8	ca. 4½	ca. 10	Half pint
	Lagers	7-9½	4-5½	9-12½	
	Stout	5-8	3-4½	6½-10	
	Guinness	ca. 8	4½	10	
	Strong Ales ("Barley Wines")	15-19	8½-11	13-17	"Nip" (⅓ pint)
Cider	Commercial	6-9	3½-5	8-11	½ pint
	Farmhouse	Very variable 4½-(20?)	4½- (11½?)	11-(50?)	Pint
Table Wines*	Still	11-27	6½-15½	6-14	
	Claret, Burgundy	ca. 19	ca. 11	ca. 10	4-oz. glass
	Hock	ca. 16	ca. 9	ca. 8	
	Sparkling (Champagne)	ca. 17	ca. 10	ca. 9	
Fortified Wines and Aperitifs*	Sherry, Port, Madeira,	35-36	20-21	9-10	2-oz. glass
	Vermouths & Aperitifs (Dubonnet, etc.)	30-31	17-18	8-9	
Spirits	Whisky, Gin, Rum, Brandy, Vodka†	70	40	7½	English "single" (5/6 fl. oz.)
				10	Formerly customary Scottish "single" (1/22 of bottle)
Liqueurs	Alcoholic strengths vary widely	ca. 25-95	ca. 15-55	Up to 10 grams, assuming a glass holding one English "single" spirit measure	

* For fiscal purposes, wines are divided into "light" (*i.e.* table—up to 25 per cent. proof, or 27 per cent. for Commonwealth wines), "heavy (*i.e.* fortified—above 25/27 per cent. proof) and "sparkling." Within each type the duty payable and therefore the price does not depend on the alcoholic strength.

† Some cut-price spirits ("cocktail gin," etc.) may be only 65 per cent. proof. Schnapps (Scandinavian "Akavit") may be up to 75 per cent proof. Imported vodkas, and also American spirits and spirit-based "cordials" may be over 90 per cent. proof.

per cent. proof," or "70 under proof"—all meaning the same thing Similarly, a strength of, say, 120 proof would be given as "120 degrees (or per cent.) proof" or (more usually) "20 over proof." In Great Britain, spirits are normally bottled and sold at a strength of 70 degrees proof, which corresponds almost exactly to 33 per cent. of alcohol weight/weight or 40 per cent. volume/volume. Absolute, or pure alcohol is 175·35 degrees proof in Great Britain and 200 degrees proof in the U.S.A.

British proof strength is also used throughout the British Commonwealth and in ex-Commonwealth countries (including South Africa).

All other countries of the world, with a few unimportant exceptions, express the alcoholic strength of drinks as per cent. volume/volume. Thus, for example, a French *vin ordinaire* labelled as "9·5°" will contain 9·5 per cent. of alcohol volume/volume.

The table on p. 5 gives the approximate alcoholic strengths of some of the liquors normally consumed in Great Britain.

WARNING

About the only completely unqualified statement which can safely be made about the absorption and effects of alcohol is that when a sufficient quantity has been absorbed the drinker will show the familiar symptoms of intoxication, and that if no more alcohol is consumed the effects will gradually wear off again.

Vast numbers of researches have been made, and their results published in thousands of scientific papers, on the physiology pharmacology, distribution in the body and effects of alcohol. Many of these have produced extremely interesting, valuable and significant results. It should however always be remembered that the personal factor—the individual characteristics of the drinker—represents the most important single variable in all of these experiments. Some experimenters have tended to forget this fact, and have sometimes drawn general conclusions which were simply not warranted by the comparatively small body of evidence upon which they were based. The results of any experiment based on a limited number of subjects can at the most, in the absence of conflicting results, be tentatively accepted as valid.

We must not nevertheless throw out the baby of common sense with the bath water of incompletely verified results. To take a crude but, we hope adequate, analogy, although the human skull varies very widely indeed in thickness and strength, that fact does not justify any doubt about the outcome in the case of an unfortunate individual who falls on his head from a tenth-floor window.

CHAPTER 2

THE ABSORPTION AND ELIMINATION OF ALCOHOL

FOR alcohol to produce its well-known effects, desired or otherwise, it must reach the brain. To do so after having been drunk it must first pass into the bloodstream by absorption through the walls of the alimentary tract. This is a straightforward physico-chemical process of diffusion, which will continue as long as the concentration of alcohol within the alimentary tract is higher than that in the blood.

The alcohol first passes in this way from the stomach and duodenum into the portal vein, the blood in which carries it to the liver. This blood then passes from the liver to the right side of the heart, thence to the lungs, back as arterial blood to the left side of the heart, and from there into the general systemic circulation, by which means it eventually reaches the brain. As the liver has also its own supply of arterial (oxygenated) blood, the alcohol in the general systemic circulation also reaches the liver again by that route.

As soon as any alcohol is present in the bloodstream, various mechanisms for its removal come into action, by far the most important of these being destructive oxidation in the liver. As we have just seen, the alcohol reaches the liver immediately after absorption, so that its destruction begins even before it reaches the general circulation. The overall rate of its removal is practically constant, and is considerably less than the rate at which alcohol initially enters the blood by diffusion. Therefore, a graph in which blood-alcohol concentration is plotted against time (the well-known *blood-alcohol curve*) should show:

1. A sharply rising portion, during which absorption is faster than elimination. (The *absorption phase*.)

2. A point of inflexion, which represents the moment at which the gradually diminishing rate of absorption becomes slower than the constant rate of elimination. (The maximum or *peak*.)

3. A gently falling portion, which is approximately a straight line and represents the elimination of alcohol from the bloodstream at a constant rate. (The *elimination phase*.)

The "typical," idealised blood-alcohol curve therefore appears as shown in fig. 1, and two actual experimentally determined ones are shown in fig. 2.

EXPRESSION OF BLOOD-ALCOHOL CONCENTRATIONS

In any meaningful discussion of the effects of alcohol and its distribution in the body, it is necessary to specify the actual concentrations in the blood and other body fluids. These concentrations will always be vastly smaller than those in the alcoholic drinks mentioned in Chapter 1. (The concentration of alcohol in the blood of

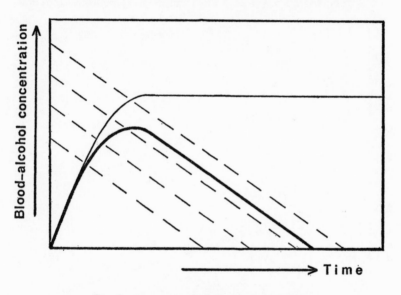

Fig. 1. THE BLOOD-ALCOHOL CURVE: THEORY

Alcohol is rapidly absorbed from the alimentary tract into the bloodstream. If there were no mechanism for its removal, its concentration in the blood would therefore rise to and remain at a level determined by the quantity absorbed (thin solid line). However, in fact oxidation in the liver removes it at a nearly constant rate, so that the blood concentration would fall regularly from any given initial concentration (sloping broken lines). The resultant of these two opposing processes is the *blood-alcohol curve* (thick solid line).

a very drunk man is about one-tenth of that in a very weak beer.) It is therefore convenient to use different units from those suitable for alcoholic drinks.

In general three systems are or have been used throughout the world.

1. A percentage figure, as used in the U.S.A. and (formerly) in Great Britain. This has the advantage that everyone is familiar with percentages, but it has two disadvantages:

(a) The figure is ambiguous unless it is clearly specified whether it is weight/weight, weight/volume or volume/volume. (See p. 3.) Per cent. weight/volume is most commonly used, and may be assumed if not stated. However, errors have arisen from failure to be specific on this point.

(b) The figure is always a fraction (*i.e.* less than 1·0) and often indeed has a zero after the decimal point. Serious mis-

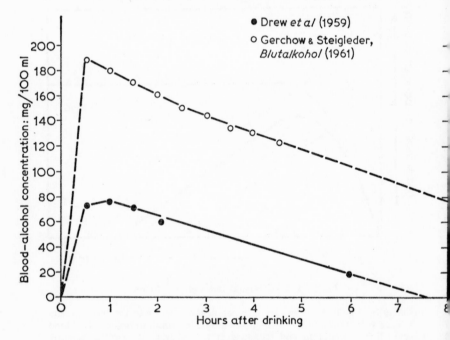

Fig. 2. THE BLOOD-ALCOHOL CURVE: PRACTICE

Two actual blood-alcohol curves, for a large and a small amount of alcohol, based on figures recorded from experiments performed in Germany and Britain respectively.

takes could therefore arise from printing errors leading to the misplacement of the decimal point or to the presence of too few or too many zeros.

2. A figure expressing grams (of alcohol) per litre (of blood or other body fluid). This is therefore parts per thousand, weight/volume, and is commonly used on the Continent with the designation "pro mille." This system is convenient, but suffers also from the disadvantage that a decimal point almost always has to be used.

3. The system now general in this country and adopted by statute, in which the weight/volume concentrations are expressed in milligrammes per 100 millilitres. The use of such units may be prima facie less familiar, but the system has the immense advantage that the relevant concentrations are always fairly large whole numbers with which it is never necessary to use decimal points. This system will be adopted throughout in this book.

There seems to be little hope of a uniform system being adopted throughout the world. One of the present writers was, as it happens, secretary of a working party which met to discuss this very matter at two international conferences, and the party finally disbanded with the conviction that each country was too firmly wedded to its own system for any change to be practicable.

Should it ever be necessary to convert from one system to another, the following table shows the simple arithmetic necessary.

To convert From To	Milligrammes per 100 millilitres	Parts per 1,000 (Pro mille)	Per cent. w/v
Milligrammes per 100 millilitres		Divide by 100	Divide by 1,000
Parts per 1,000 (Pro mille)	Multiply by 100		Divide by 10
Per cent. w/v	Multiply by 1,000	Multiply by 10	

THE BLOOD-ALCOHOL CURVE: ABSORPTION AND THE "PEAK"

In the present context, the three most important quantities of which the blood-alcohol curve is an expression are:

1. The time until the peak—that is, the time after drinking starts at which the highest concentration is reached.

2. The concentration at the peak—that is, the highest concentration reached in the blood after drinking.

3. The rate of fall of the blood-alcohol concentration after the peak.

As 1. and 2. are closely connected, and indeed to some extent interdependent, they will be considered together. It should be obvious from what has been said above that there will be at least some connection between time-to-peak and peak height; if absorption is rapid, the maximum quantity of alcohol will pass into the blood before any significant degree of elimination has taken place; whereas, if absorption is slow, a significant quantity of alcohol will have been eliminated from the blood before absorption is complete.

To begin with, the theoretical maximum possible peak concentration is easily calculated, provided that one:

1. Assumes that all the alcohol has been absorbed before any significant degree of elimination has taken place.

2. Assumes that the alcohol is uniformly distributed throughout all the water in the body.

3. Knows the total quantity of water in the body.

4. Knows the total quantity of alcohol consumed.

This subject was extensively studied in the pioneering work of E. Widmark in Sweden (1914 onwards), and he produced the simple formula:

$$a = c \times p \times r$$

where a is the total amount of alcohol taken, c is the peak concentration in the blood, p is the weight of the drinker, and r is a factor derived from the proportion of the total body mass over which the alcohol can be distributed. r is in fact the ratio of the water content of the entire body to that of the circulating blood. Widmark himself referred to it as the "reduced body weight," but it is now more commonly referred to simply as the "Widmark factor."

Blood contains 80-85 per cent. of water; 83 per cent. may be taken as a fair average figure. The proportion of water in the body as a whole depends on age, sex and body habit, and varies from slightly under 50 to slightly over 60 per cent. (It is not necessary here to specify whether these percentages are weight/weight, weight/volume or volume/volume, since the specific gravities of blood and of the body as a whole may be assumed for the purpose of this calculation to be the same as that of water.) Fat does not absorb alcohol to any significant extent (see, *e.g. Grüner* 1959), and fatty tissue and bone contain less water than other tissues; the combined effects of these facts is that the proportion of water in the body is higher in the young than in the old, in the lean than in the obese, and in men than in women (whose bodies contain a higher proportion of fat). The theoretical values of r will therefore be $^{60}/_{83}$ (*i.e.* 0·72) for a body containing 60 per cent. of water, and $^{50}/_{83}$ (*i.e.* 0·60) for a body containing 50 per cent. of water. The mean values of r found experimentally by Widmark himself were 0·68 for men and 0·55 for women. These figures agree reasonably well with the theoretically derived ones, and have been substantially confirmed by many subsequent experiments.

If therefore, to take one simple example, an 11-stone man drinks two double whiskies, his theoretical peak blood concentration will be given by (turning the Widmark equation around):

$$c = \frac{a}{p \times r}$$

Since a single whisky contains approximately 7·5 grams of alcohol (p. 5), a will be 30 grams. p (11 stones=154 lbs.) is approximately 70 kilograms. Therefore, taking r as 0·68,

$$c = \frac{30}{70 \times 0.68}$$
$$= 0.063 \text{ per cent. w/v}$$

Any experimentally determined blood-alcohol curve will always (for an initially sober subject) start a zero, rise to a maximum and fall to zero again. However, we have already seen that destruction in the liver begins even before the alcohol enters the general circulation. Therefore the peak concentration can never be quite as high as that given by the above simple theoretical calculation, and in practice it may if absorption is slow be very considerably lower.

The whole course of the curve may also show considerable fluctuations and thereby depart from the simple idealised form of fig. 1.

We will consider briefly the factors which may modify the course of the blood-alcohol curve and the peak concentration resulting from the consumption of a given amount of alcohol.

Duration of drinking

It is obvious that, if the drink is taken sufficiently slowly, the alcohol can be eliminated as fast, or nearly as fast, as it enters the blood, and the highest concentration actually reached may be only a small fraction of that calculated as above. If, to anticipate (*cf.* pp. 17-19), we assume that an average man can eliminate the equivalent of one single whisky per hour, then, if the two doubles of the above example were taken as four singles at hourly intervals, the blood concentration would never rise above that corresponding to a single whisky—approximately 18 milligrammes/100 millilitres. As a rough-and-ready rule of thumb, it can be taken that any drinking time longer than an hour will significantly reduce the peak blood-alcohol concentration below that reached if the drink were taken all at once.

Nature of liquor consumed

There has been a great deal of experimental work on this point, and the results have not always been free of contradictions. However it can be taken as established that:

1. In general, up to a certain point (but see 2., below) the more concentrated the alcohol the faster it is absorbed and the higher, therefore, is the peak concentration.

2. The maximum rate of absorption appears to occur when the drink contains somewhere about 20 per cent. volume/volume of alcohol. Newman (cited *Drew et al.* 1959) suggests that higher concentrations than this (*i.e.* neat spirits on an empty stomach) irritate the gastro-intestinal tissues and cause the absorptive surfaces to be coated and protected by the secretion of mucus. He also suggests that the motility of the stomach is decreased. *Wayne* (1962) states that concentrated alcohol tends to inhibit the opening of the pyloric sphincter between the stomach and the duodenum; both this and Newman's second suggestion would mean that the passage of the alcohol into the duodenum (where it is absorbed most rapidly—see p. 16) is delayed, so that the rate of absorption falls.

3. The alcohol is absorbed rather more rapidly from carbonated (sparkling) drinks—which is why one gets a bigger "kick"

from champagne than from a still wine of equal alcoholic strength.

4. Absorption is much delayed or reduced by the presence of soluble nutrients in the drink. In particular, absorption is much slower from beer, which contains various carbohydrates, etc., than from spirits diluted with water or soda to the same actual alcoholic strength. (See, for example, *Mallach* 1966.) This effect is so pronounced that, if the alcohol is drunk as beer, especially a heavy beer, the peak blood-alcohol concentration may be as little as one-third of the theoretical maximum for the alcohol taken.

The presence or absence, and nature, of food in the stomach

It is a well-known fact that alcohol taken with food usually has less effect than that taken on an empty stomach, but, if one seeks to go beyond that very general statement, the experimental results which have been published are, to say the least, by no means always in agreement.

The results of a series of experiments published by *Abele* and *Kropp* in 1958 may be taken as typical, though not necessarily exactly applicable on all occasions. There were ninety-six tests, in which the subjects were given doses of alcohol ranging from 45 to 150 grams, and were divided into three groups, according to when the last large meal was taken, namely: more than 6 hours before drinking, 3-6 hours before drinking, and less than 3 hours before drinking. Within 45 minutes after drinking, the blood-alcohol levels of the third group had risen on the average to only one-half of those shown by the first group, for the same quantities of alcohol per unit of body weight.

It should perhaps be noted that results such as these really apply only to alcohol consumed as wines or spirits; the absorption from beer is in any case so much retarded that the additional effect of food is relatively much less important.

The evidence as to which types of food are most effective in this respect is somewhat conflicting, and the claims which have been made are possibly exaggerated and certainly not always disinterested. Claims have also been made for the high effectiveness of, *e.g.* milk, olive oil and mashed potatoes. It does however seem to be pretty well established that fats, including vegetable oils, are particularly effective in this respect.

Eating *after* absorption is complete cannot of course affect its rate. It has been stated in a recent German paper (*Etzler et al.* 1968) that food taken after the blood-alcohol peak will accelerate the elimination *after* absorption of alcohol previously drunk on an empty stomach. The effect was however very small and hardly significant, and was detectable only when the blood alcohol had already fallen to a low level. In practice therefore it can be assumed that eating or not eating makes no difference to the course of the blood-alcohol curve once absorption is complete.

Physiological factors

When all of the above factors have been taken into account, there will still remain, as a factor influencing the rate of absorption, the anatomical and physiological characteristics of the drinker. There are probably variations, both between different people and between different times for the same person, in such things as stomach-wall permeability and the blood supply to the alimentary tract. These causes affecting the absorption rate are, however, not open to experimental investigation, and their combined effects must simply appear as the scatter of the results normal in all biological experimentation.

However, the most important factor of this type, of which there has been some investigation, is the rate at which the stomach contents pass into the duodenum. It has been shown that absorption through the duodenal wall is much faster than through the stomach wall. Therefore the overall rate of absorption will depend on how fast and how soon the stomach contents pass into the duodenum, and this in turn will depend on the opening and closing of the pyloric sphincter, which controls the opening between these two organs. This also accounts for the well-known fact that persons who have undergone gastrectomy are more easily and more quickly affected by alcohol drunk.

This factor may well account for the irregular course sometimes shown by experimentally determined blood-alcohol curves (*Ponsold* 1965); the sudden passage into the duodenum of alcohol-laden liquid in the stomach would be expected to result in a temporarily raised rate of absorption. It has also been shown that in certain circumstances the intake of food may, contrary to the normal rule described above, temporarily raise the absorption rate, since its entry into a stomach empty except for some alcohol-laden liquid may cause the closed sphincter to open.

THE BLOOD-ALCOHOL CURVE; ELIMINATION

Oxidation in the liver, which eliminates 30 per cent. or more of the alcohol absorbed, takes place in two stages:

$$\text{alcohol} \rightarrow \text{acetaldehyde} \rightarrow \text{acetic acid,}$$

each stage being catalysed by the appropriate enzyme, that responsible for the first stage of the conversion being known as *alcohol dehydrogenase* (ADH). As the second stage of the conversion is normally much faster than the first, the concentration of acetaldehyde in the blood during elimination remains minute. (The action of drugs given to alcoholics for aversion therapy is to block the second stage of the conversion, so that the accumulation of rather toxic acetaldehyde makes the drinker feel very ill.) The end product, acetic acid, is finally oxidised to carbon dioxide and water. Alcohol may therefore be regarded as a food in the sense that its metabolism produces energy, and it can replace to some extent energy-giving foods such as fats and carbohydrates.

The other routes of elimination are by excretion of unchanged alcohol which has diffused into the urine via the kidneys, into expired breath via the lungs, and into sweat via the sweat glands. All of these taken together probably do not in normal circumstances account for more than 5 per cent. of the alcohol ingested; it is fallacious to suppose that alcohol can be got rid of to any significant extent by "sweating it out" or by copious urination, since the greatest quantities of urine or sweat that can be produced are barely significant in comparison with the total quantity of water in the body. To a first approximation, therefore, the elimination of alcohol from the blood will proceed at a constant rate determined by the oxidative capacity of the liver enzymes, and not affected by the peak blood-alcohol level reached.

Numerous series of experiments have been made to determine this rate of fall, and the results have agreed remarkably closely. *Elbel & Schleyer* (p. 61) give a mean value based on numerous tests made during the years 1930-55 which, converted to our notation for concentration, corresponds to a fall of 13·8 milligrammes/ 100 millilitres per hour. *Jacobsen* (1952) gives 15 ± 5 milligrammes/ 100 millilitres per hour. Some more recent results (all expressed as milligrammes/100 millilitres per hour) are:

Drew et al. (1959): approximately 16 (mean)

Coldwell & Smith (1959): 13 ± 5

Ponsold & Heite (1960): Mean 17·2, with scatter of "up to 50 per cent." on either side of the mean

Foster, Schulz & Starck (1961): Range from 12 to 28; mean 16 and modal (*i.e.* most common) value 13

Schleyer & Wichmann (1962): 15 ± 7

Bonnichsen, Dimberg & Sjöberg (1964): 14 to 20

Taking all of these results into account, it would seem that where a most probable rate of fall of blood alcohol has to be assumed, we should take 15 milligrammes/100 millilitres per hour, but that we cannot assume that the rate will not be as low as 10 (or even less in extreme cases) or as high as 25 (or even more in a few extreme cases.)

These rates of elimination correspond, for a man of average weight (11 stones or 70 kilograms), to the disappearance of between approximately 5 and 13 grams of alcohol per hour, with a most probable figure in the neighbourhood of 7. This last figure is almost exactly the amount of alcohol contained in a single whisky (Ch. 1).

Although a constant rate of disappearance of blood alcohol, which accords reasonably well with the experimental results, should be assumed in practice if any calculations have to be made, careful and reliable experimenters have found some evidence that the rate varies slightly with blood-alcohol level, age and degree of habituation to alcohol. A good many years ago, Goldberg of the Karolinska Institute in Stockholm, probably the leading authority in this field, showed that the rate tended to be slightly greater for high levels. More recently, it has been found that the rate seems to be slightly greater in the old than in the young, and is considerably greater in alcoholics than in non-drinkers or occasional drinkers. (*Schweitzer* 1968; *Bonnichsen et al.* 1968. Bonnichsen, who is Director of the State Laboratory doing the blood-alcohol analyses for the whole of Sweden, is a most trustworthy authority.)

There is a reasonable theoretical explanation for a greater rate at very high levels. Since diffusion into the breath and urine is a physico-chemical process of equilibration, the *concentrations* of alcohol in these two fluids will depend on that in the blood, and therefore the absolute quantities removed in that way per unit of time will be higher, the higher is the concentration in the blood. On the other hand, oxidation will remove the same absolute quantity per unit of time. Therefore, removal via the breath and urine will be proportionately the more effective the higher is the blood-alcohol level. *Lundquist and Wolthers* (1958) have suggested that at blood-alcohol levels of the order of 300 milligrammes/100 millilitres elimination via the breath and urine may represent as much as 15 per cent. of the total, as opposed to about 3 per cent. for a blood-alcohol level of 50 milligrammes/100 millilitres.

At very low blood-alcohol levels the concentration of alcohol in the blood passing through the liver may also not be sufficient fully to saturate the oxidative capacity of the enzymes available, thereby reducing the absolute rate of destruction. This effect will however appear only at blood-alcohol levels too low to be of any significance in our present context. (See *e.g. Lester* 1962.)

OTHER POSSIBLE EFFECTS ON THE BLOOD-ALCOHOL CURVE

Drugs

There is a certain amount of somewhat inconclusive experimental evidence about the effects of other drugs on the blood-alcohol curve. *Casier et al.* (1966) found that the simultaneous administration of nialamide (an anti-depressant) or chlorpromazine (a tranquilliser) reduced the blood ethanol during the first hour after drinking, but not thereafter. Most other workers have however found that, whatever the subjective or behavioural effects produced by other drugs (see Chapter 9), they have had no effect on the blood-alcohol curve. For example, *Goldberg* (1965) found no such effect for either amphetamine or for ten different tranquillisers. In the particular case of caffeine (tea or coffee), although some workers have claimed to find effects on the curve, these have been at the most minimal or transitory. Insulin has been found to accelerate the metabolism of alcohol in dogs (*Newman et al.* 1959), but this effect does not appear to have been tested experimentally in Man—no doubt for the obvious reason that such an experiment would be extremely dangerous.

Muscular activity

Some workers have claimed that strenuous work does, others that it does not, increase the rate of alcohol metabolism. (See references cited by *Pawan* 1968.) An increased rate of respiration will of course *slightly* increase elimination (see above), but there is no very conclusive evidence that muscular activity increases the actual rate of metabolism *per se*. The most recent experiments (Pawan, *loc. cit.* in Appendix 1), in which the subjects undertook really strenuous exercise (a 3-mile run or a 1,000-yard swim), produced no evidence of increased elimination. (See also *Elbel & Schleyer*, pp. 92-94; *Krauland, Mallach, Mellerowicz & Müller* 1965; *Krauland* 1966.)

Sleep: unconsciousness

The rate of alcohol elimination is unchanged during sleep or unconsciousness. *Elbel & Schleyer*, pp. 92-94; *Apel* 1960.)

Vomiting

It is obvious that if vomiting occurs whilst there is still alcohol in the stomach, the alcohol ejected in the vomit cannot be absorbed and the blood-alcohol level will not therefore rise as high as if vomiting had not occurred. Vomiting, if it occurs before the peak has been reached, does appear to produce some small changes in the blood-alcohol curve, which can be ascribed to a changed rate of absorption of the alcohol remaining in the alimentary tract and not ejected with the vomit, but the evidence on this point is conflicting and unclear. There is no evidence that vomiting occurring after the peak—during the elimination phase—has any effect on the curve. It is of interest, incidentally, that the intravenous injection of alcohol can produce vomiting, which shows that it may be a reaction of the nervous system rather than a purely local effect. (*Elbel & Schleyer*, pp. 97-99; *Wayne* 1963 Discussion; *Ditt* 1963.)

Blood loss

The loss of up to 10 per cent. of the total blood in the body produces no change in the course of the blood-alcohol curve. (*Elbel & Schleyer*, pp. 102-103; *Ditt & Schulze* 1962.)

Various diseases

There is a limited amount of experimental evidence that neither moderate liver dysfunction (*Elbel & Schleyer* p. 55; *Kulpe & Mallach* 1961), nor anaemia (*Schleyer* 1966), nor diabetes (*Coldwell & Grant* 1963—II) has any effect on the blood-alcohol curve.

"ENDOGENOUS" ALCOHOL

Traces of ethanol occurring as intermediate products of normal metabolism were at one time thought to be present in the body.

However, it is now certain that these, if they occur at all, are much too minute to be of any forensic significance whatsoever. (See *Lester* 1961, modified by *Lester* 1962; *Harger* 1965; *Harger & Forney* 1967.)

INGESTION OF ALCOHOL BY INHALATION

It has occasionally been suggested that alcohol present in the body could have been inhaled as vapour—for example, by brewery workers, users of paints and varnishes containing ethanol as a solvent, etc.

The relationship between alcohol vapour in the lungs and alcohol in the blood will be discussed again below (pp. 34-37). The earlier work on absorption by inhalation is summarised by *Elbel & Schleyer* (pp. 11-12). The results of this are very inconclusive. It can however be asserted that blood-alcohol concentrations significant in the present context will never have been produced by the inhalation of alcohol vapour, since high concentrations of alcohol vapour are unbearably irritating to breathe, and the highest blood-alcohol level which could ever in normal circumstances be produced in this way seems to lie between 10 and 20 milligrammes/100 millilitres. (*Elbel & Schleyer.*)

"SOBERERS"

From time to time various drugs are reported and advertised with claims that taking them speeds up the elimination of alcohol from the blood and promotes a quicker return to sobriety.

There are theoretical reasons for supposing that ingestion of fructose (fruit sugar, laevulose) could accelerate the oxidative destruction of alcohol. In practice, however, the amount which has to be taken to produce any significant effect, when combined with alcohol, leads to nausea, vomiting, belly-aches and other unpleasant symptoms. (See *Elbel & Schleyer*, pp. 77-80; *Lester* 1965.)

Some of the preparations which have been marketed have been scientifically tested. Two German ones ("Promill-Ex" and "Jatroneural") were found to have no effect on the blood-alcohol curve. (*Burger* 1959; *Osterhaus & Johannsmeier* 1964.) More recently, a preparation containing fructose ("Laevoral C") has also been tested (*Camps & Robinson* 1968). Although there was some evidence that taking this along with alcohol led to slightly lower blood-alcohol peaks, there did not seem to be any effect on the subsequent rate of elimination, and the conclusion was reached that the preparation "is unlikely to be of value to the apparently healthy social drinker who wishes to drive home after an evening's entertainment without infringing the law." The same effects have been reported for "Alkohol Minus" (ALMI), a similar German preparation. (*Rauschke* 1968.)

CHAPTER 3

DISTRIBUTION

ALCOHOL which has diffused into the bloodstream is carried by it to all the tissues of the body, and diffuses into them also. Eventually it is uniformly distributed throughout the water in the body, and the concentration in any tissue is then proportional to the water content of that tissue; how quickly this state of equilibrium is reached in any particular tissue, however, depends upon the blood supply to it.

This question of distribution is important in the present context because chemical analyses for alcohol are not or cannot always be made on the blood itself, but on some other body fluid, yet it is always the blood-alcohol concentration which we seek to know. The ultimately important quantity is of course the level of alcohol in the brain. This however must obviously remain unknown in living persons, and our limited knowledge of the relationship between blood alcohol and brain alcohol is derived either from animal experiments, the results of which do not necessarily apply *in toto* to Man, or from analyses when the opportunity presents itself of samples from dead bodies, the results of which may be falsified by post-mortem changes and are in any case not necessarily applicable to the living. Experimental observations on the effects of various body-alcohol levels are always therefore related to blood-alcohol levels, whether these are determined directly or by analysis of some other body fluid.

"Blood-alcohol concentration" is not however even by itself a completely unambiguous term, since there is ample evidence that during the absorption phase the concentration differs in different parts of the circulation. (See *e.g. Payne et al.* 1966.) It has been shown both by animal and by human experiments that during this period the concentration in venous blood lags behind that in the arterial, with that in capillary blood occupying an intermediate position, possibly rather nearer to the arterial than to the venous concentration. (Arterial blood never of course reaches the forensic chemist for analysis in the present context; what he receives is either capillary blood from a skin puncture or venous blood taken by syringe.) The time required for the venous to catch up with the arterial concentration appears to be most usually between 30 minutes and 2 hours.

This differential during absorption is not hard to explain. The highest concentration of alcohol presumably occurs in blood flowing from the sites of absorption at the wall of the alimentary tract. This blood then, as explained in Chapter 2, passes into the general circulation, and any alcohol in it diffuses into the tissues, slowly into the muscles and rapidly into organs such as the brain or kidneys. The same blood returning in the veins after passing through the capillaries will therefore show a lower concentration. As diffusion into the muscles is a rather slow process compared with absorption from the alimentary tract, the arterial blood concentration will during this phase be rising faster than diffusion can maintain the equilibrium.

Once the peak has been passed, the blood-alcohol level then changes almost entirely through the (relatively slow) destruction in the liver, and as this is slow enough for diffusion into or from the muscles nearly to keep pace with it, a state of equilibrium is maintained throughout the whole circulation—in fact, throughout the whole body. (The recent very precise experiments of Payne and his colleagues [*op. cit.* in Appendix 1] have, it is true, shown that during the elimination phase the venous alcohol concentration may be slightly higher than the arterial, which they explain as showing that elimination by excretion and metabolism is not in fact quite as rapid as diffusion back from the tissues into the blood. This difference is however quite small, and can legitimately be disregarded for our present purpose.) In short, there is general agreement that after not more than 2 hours from the end of drinking, circulation equilibrium can be assumed, and that from then on there will be for practical purposes a uniform blood-alcohol level which can be determined by the analysis of blood taken from any source.

As alcohol diffuses out of the bloodstream it naturally appears also in all the secretions, and it has been amply demonstrated that it can be detected in every accessible body fluid other than blood— sweat, saliva, urine, milk and expired breath, to name the most important. However, only two of these are of other than academic interest for us here: namely, urine and expired breath.

ALCOHOL IN THE URINE

The relationship between blood alcohol and urine alcohol, though fundamentally a fairly straightforward one, can be quite complex in its practical implications.

It depends upon two factors:

1. Urine consists for our present purpose entirely of water; its other constituents are all in solution and may be disregarded. Blood on the other hand contains about 15-20 per cent. of suspended solids.

2. The blood-alcohol concentration is changing continuously, either up or down. Urine, on the other hand, although also continuously secreted by the kidneys from this ever-changing blood, is stored in the bladder and excreted in "batches" in each of which the alcohol concentration depends upon and reflects the average blood concentration whilst it was being secreted.

The effect of the first factor is that for blood and urine in diffusion equilibrium, (*i.e.* at the moment of secretion in the kidney).

$$\frac{\text{Urine-alcohol concentration}}{\text{Blood-alcohol concentration}} = \frac{\text{Water content of urine}}{\text{Water content of blood}}$$

$$= \frac{100 \text{ per cent.}}{83 \text{ per cent. (average)}}$$

$$= 1{\cdot}20.$$

This figure cannot of course be experimentally checked in Man, since the urine is not accessible at the moment of its secretion in the kidney. It has however been reasonably confirmed by animal experiments.

However, because of the second factor mentioned above, one would *a priori* not expect the same ratio to be found with samples taken under normal everyday circumstances. In general, a "batch" of urine which has been secreted during the absorption phase will show a lower concentration than that corresponding to the blood level at the moment the urine is passed, and conversely a batch secreted during the elimination phase will show a higher concen-

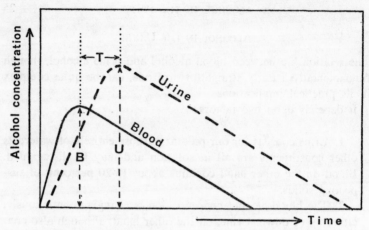

Fig. 3. BLOOD ALCOHOL AND URINE ALCOHOL: THEORY

As explained in the text, the "peak" concentration of alcohol in the urine is higher than that in the blood, but is reached later. Normally, the urine peak is about one-third higher than the blood (*i.e.*, U/B=4/3, approximately), and the time lag between the peaks (T) is around ½-1 hour.

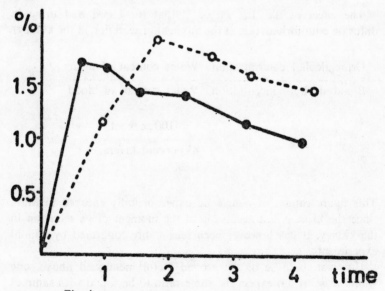

Fig. 4. BLOOD ALCOHOL AND URINE ALCOHOL: PRACTICE

An actual pair of blood-alcohol and urine-alcohol curves, determined for a test subject weighing 175 lb. (80 kilograms) who had drunk 102 grams of alcohol as whisky during 32 minutes. The figures on the horizontal axis are hours, and those on the vertical axis blood alcohol as parts per thousand (1·0=100 mg/100 ml).

tration. Also, because of the time-lag between the secretion and the passing of urine, the urine peak will occur later than the blood peak. The general form of the relationship between urine and blood alcohol levels is shown diagrammatically in fig. 3. Experimentally, the urine peak has been found to occur up to an hour after the blood peak. (Fig. 4. See also *Payne et al.* 1966.)

Such results seem to show that the bladder wall is not permeable by alcohol; if it was, a diffusion equilibrium would be established across it and the blood and urine concentrations would always be equivalent. This is prima facie surprising, since other body membranes are permeable by alcohol and since various diffusible sub-

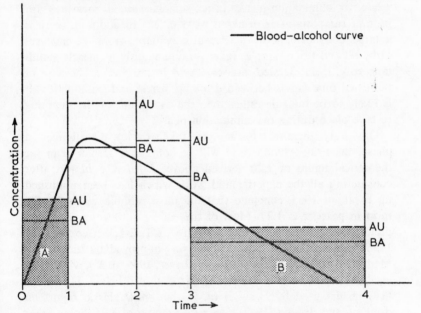

Fig. 5. BLOOD AND URINE ALCOHOL LEVELS

The urine-alcohol level affords a reasonably good measure of the blood-alcohol level if, but only if, the urine analysed has been secreted during the elimination phase of the blood-alcohol curve. In the hypothetical case here, it is assumed that urine is passed at times 0, 1, 2, 3 and 4. Then the alcohol concentrations in the urines passed at times 1-4 (AU) will in each case be about 4/3 of the *average* blood concentrations (BA) during the periods (0-1, 1-2, etc.) since the previous emptying of the bladder. Hence ¾ of the urine concentration at times 2 and 3 will provide a fair estimate of the blood concentrations just before these times. However, analysis of urine passed at 1 will give much too low a blood figure (case A), and conversely of urine passed at 4 much too high a blood figure (case B). The latter case is however most unlikely ever to arise in practice. See also figs. 6, 7 and 8.

stances, including alcohol, injected into the bladder can be detected subsequently in the blood. The truth appears to be that, although the bladder wall may be permeable by alcohol to some extent, it is so poorly supplied with blood vessels that the interchange across it of alcohol between the blood and the bladder contents is too slow to have any significant effect in this connection.

The earlier experimenters did not always realise clearly the necessity for making a distinction between absorption-phase and elimination-phase urine; in any case, the actual time of the blood peak was rarely known. However, since the absorption phase lasts a much shorter time than the elimination, most published results probably relate to elimination-phase urine, unless special measures for prompt sampling after drinking were taken. In addition, there is a large body of experimental results available from the analyses of blood and urine samples taken simultaneously, or nearly simultaneously, from arrested motorists, and in these cases, because of the usual time lapses between drinking, arrest and examination, it is likely to be the rule rather than the exception for the sampling to take place during the elimination phase.

Obviously, therefore, for samples taken during the elimination phase, the urine: blood ratio will be somewhat greater than the theoretical figure of 1.20 derived above. *Elbel & Schleyer*, after considering all the experimental work which had been published up to about 1955, conclude that the most reliable value for the ratio in practice is 1.27. Most of the earlier authorities, however, preferred the marginally higher figure of 1.32-1.33 (see *Nickolls* 1956), and this is the figure which was approved by the British Medical Association (*The Drinking Driver*, 1965, p. 29), with, however, an important qualification to be mentioned below. The analytical results used by *Drew et al.* in their now classic report on drinking and driving (1959) give a mean ratio of 1.25. Some other published results are:

Coldwell & Smith (*loc. cit.* in Appendix 1 1959) (Canada): mean 1.24

Lundquist (1961) (Denmark): mean 1.35

Bonnichsen et al. (1964) (Sweden): approximately 1.3

Morgan (1965) (Northern Ireland): mean calculated from published results 1.36

Saury et al. (1966) (France): mean 1.35

Payne et al. (1967) (England): mean 1.44

What ratio should be assumed in the circumstances of traffic-law enforcement, where the times cannot be controlled as they are in laboratory experiments, may of course be a matter of importance, and was indeed of great importance in this country before the operation of the Road Safety Act 1967, when the bulk of the specimens analysed were urine ones. The forensic science service in general used for conversion of analysed urine to calculated blood figures the ratio $\frac{3}{4}$ (i.e. the reciprocal of 1.33), which was supported by the published B.M.A. recommendation and by their own extensive experience and accumulated results. This figure was also adopted in the Road Safety Act 1967, which lays down that, for the purposes of the Act only, a urine-alcohol level of 107 milligrammes/ 100 millilitres shall be deemed equivalent to a blood level of 80. ($80 \times {}^4/_3 = 107$, to the nearest unit.)

It was never of course, claimed that a urine-alcohol analysis and conversion by calculation to a blood figure necessarily gave the true level of alcohol in the blood *at the time at which the urine was passed*; it was claimed merely that the blood level must at some time before the passage of the urine have risen to a figure not less than $\frac{3}{4}$ of that found in the urine.

This assumption was however attacked from two directions— and is presumably liable still to be attacked in the event of its being made in connection with a prosecution under section 6 of the Road Traffic Act 1960 (i.e. when driving ability appears to be impaired, but the driver's blood level is below 80). The attacks used as ammunition:

(1) A long series of results published by *Froentjes* (Netherlands) in 1962. He found the mean urine:blood ratio to be almost exactly 1·5, with the bulk of his results lying between 1·0 and 2·0. He, and those using his results to attack the ${}^4/_3$ ratio, therefore recommended that in fairness to the accused a blood figure based on the highest ratio found should be used, namely half the urine figure. Although Froentjes's figure relate to a very large number of cases (nearly 10,000), it cannot be denied, in view of the numerous independent workers (including those quoted above) whose results all support a rather lower ratio, that he is the "odd man out" in this respect. Why his ratio was higher has never been satisfactorily explained; it can only be assumed that some unelucidated characteristic of Dutch police practice gave rise to a mean time between drinking and sampling different from that obtaining elsewhere.

(2) Figures such as those published by *Morgan* (Northern Ireland) in 1965 which showed that, under the normal conditions of traffic-law enforcement, a general assumption of a blood level ¾ of that found in the urine may produce a calculated result very different from that actually present in the blood at the time of sampling. We have already mentioned this point, but if it is felt that only the blood level at the time of sampling can be considered relevant, then it is obviously unjust if the calculated figure used is often higher than the true one. Morgan found in fact that, within reasonable limits of experimental error, the assumption of a ¾ ratio would have given the true blood figure in 44·7 per cent. of his cases, too low a figure in 22·3 per cent. and too high a figure in 33·0 per cent.

There can be little doubt that Morgan's and similar results were due to some of the urine specimens not having been wholly secreted during the post-peak elimination phase of the blood. (For example, in another set of figures published by *Stevens et al.* in 1966, which were based on samples obtained during social drinking, and in which the mean urine : blood ratio was only 1·10, almost

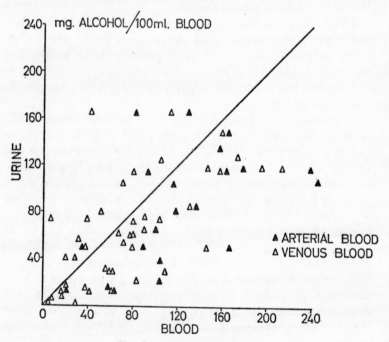

Fig. 6. THE URINE/BLOOD RATIO

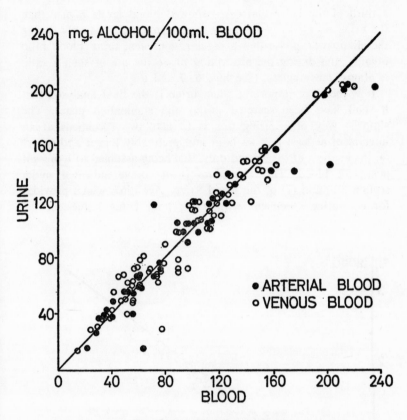

Fig. 7. THE URINE/BLOOD RATIO

In this pair of figures, which show some of the results obtained in a recent British research project, each plotted point represents a pair of urine and blood specimens taken simultaneously. The horizontal axis shows the direct blood figure, and the vertical axis the blood figure obtained by multiplying the urine figure by $\frac{3}{4}$. Hence, if the urine/blood ratio was always exactly 4/3, all the points would lie exactly on the sloping line at 45° to both axes.

In fig. 6, the specimens were taken **before** *the peak urine concentration had been reached*. There is no tendency for the ratio even to approximate to 4/3.

In fig. 7, the specimens were taken **after** *the peak urine concentration had been reached*. Nearly all the specimen pairs show a ratio lying near the 4/3 value. (See also fig. 8.)

a third of the individual cases showed blood levels *higher* than the urine ones.) As has already been mentioned, it is only during the elimination phase that a regular, consistent urine : blood ratio obtains, and during the absorption phase the use of such a ratio is almost meaningless. (See figs. 6, 7 and 8.)

It is therefore important when urine is the fluid analysed that it shall have been secreted during the elimination phase. The simplest way of ensuring this is to take two specimens at an interval of at least half an hour and preferably longer and report on the analysis of the second only, this being assumed to represent post-peak blood. This procedure is of course indicated under section 3(6) and (7) of the Road Safety Act 1967, which provides for two urine specimens within one hour being requested, the

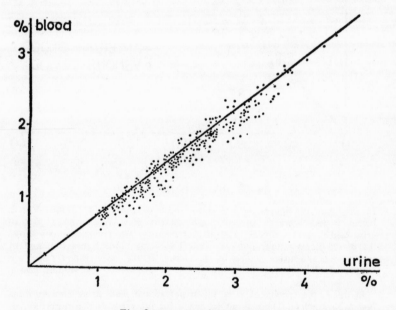

Fig. 8. THE URINE/BLOOD RATIO

Some Swedish results obtained in routine traffic-law enforcement are shown here. As in figs. 6 and 7, each point represents a pair of simultaneous urine and blood specimens, and the sloping line the ratio 4/3. In this case, however, the blood specimens were capillary ones, and the urine specimens in each instance the second of two taken about 1 hour apart. Note how closely all the ratios approximate to 4/3. (See also fig. 7.)

former of which is to be disregarded in evidence. If of course circumstances arise in which the first specimen can also be analysed, then the assumption can if necessary be confirmed. This two-specimen procedure had in fact been recommended many years ago, but a general neglect of the recommendation led the British Medical Association to re-affirm the necessity for it in 1965. (*The Drinking Driver*, pp. 31-32.)

The Act of 1967, however, in spite of this precautionary provision being contained in it, is still sometimes criticised on the ground that injustice may be done because, due to chance and personal idiosyncrasy, it may be possible for a driver to have a blood-alcohol level less than 80 milligrammes/100 millilitres when his urine-alcohol level is more than 107. This possibility cannot be gainsaid. However, the intention of the Act is (it would seem) to encourage the taking of blood rather than urine unless, exceptionally, there is some religious or medical reason to the contrary. When a level of 107 in the urine is deemed to represent a level of 80 in the blood, then there is an approximately equal chance of the actual blood level being above or below this figure. If, in order to prove a blood level greater than 80, an equivalent urine level greater than 107 was prescribed, then there would be a better than even chance of a driver who opted to give urine, but whose blood figure slightly exceeded 80, showing a urine level less than the prescribed figure and therefore escaping conviction under the Act. This would naturally and inevitably lead to urine being chosen as a "soft option", and thereby to the apparent intention of the Act (as set out in the White Paper Road Safety Legislation 1965-66) that blood should be preferred, being defeated. (See also p. 140.)

To summarise this section, a urine-alcohol analysis may have been made:

1. Under section 1 of the Road Safety Act 1967, in which case the method by which the specimen shall have been obtained is laid down by the Act, and if the figure given by analysis exceeds 107 milligrammes/100 millilitres there is no room for argument about its significance.

2. In connection with a prosecution under section 6 of the Road Traffic Act 1960 and be of a single specimen of urine only. In that case, the blood-alcohol level at any particular material time cannot be reliably calculated. If the specimen was secreted during the absorption phase, and/or consists

partly of urine already present in the bladder before any alcohol was secreted from the bloodstream, then the calculated blood figure will be lower than that actually reached. On the other hand, if the specimen was secreted wholly in the elimination phase, the blood figure calculated from its analysis may well be higher than that actually present at or shortly before the time at which the specimen was passed. In these circumstances, it is probably wise to assume a $^2/_1$ urine : blood ratio—that is, a blood-alcohol level of half the urine figure.

3. In connection with a prosecution under section 6 of the Road Traffic Act 1960 and be of two specimens of urine taken at least half an hour apart. In that case :

(a) If the second specimen shows a concentration of the same order as that in the first, then it will most probably have been secreted at a period not far removed from the blood peak. The most probable blood level is then $\frac{3}{4}$ of the urine level, but it is again safer to take $\frac{1}{2}$, as under (2).

(b) If the second specimen shows a concentration considerably higher than that in the first, then, although the peak may well have been reached by the time that the second specimen was passed, the blood level at or before the time that the first specimen was passed cannot be reliably calculated.

(c) If the second specimen shows a concentration significantly lower than that in the first, then it will have been secreted during the elimination phase; a blood concentration $\frac{3}{4}$ of that in the urine may then be assumed.

ALCOHOL IN THE BREATH

The relationship between blood-alcohol and breath alcohol concentrations is theoretically simpler than that between blood and urine concentrations, because there is nothing in the case of breath equivalent to the urine being secreted continuously but collected in the bladder and excreted in batches. The breath-alcohol concentration should in fact reflect the continuously varying concentration of alcohol in the blood.

The excretion of alcohol in the breath is fundamentally a simple matter of physical chemistry : there is an exchange of gases between the blood and the breath through the walls of the alveoli (the

tiny air sacs of the lungs in which the respiratory passages terminate) and the vapour of any alcohol present in the blood participates
in this exchange. Therefore, assuming that equilibrium has been
reached, the concentration of alcohol vapour in the expired air
will depend simply upon the alcohol concentration in the blood
and the vapour pressure of alcohol at the body temperature.

Measurements of breath-alcohol concentrations may therefore
be used as a method of determining the alcohol levels in the blood.
This was first proposed over 40 years ago, and since then an
immense volume of experimental data has accumulated on the
subject. Breath analysis has the obvious advantage over urine
analysis that it is much quicker and that it gives the blood-alcohol
concentration at the moment of sampling and not at some earlier
time.

From the data mentioned above, especially those collected by
Liljestrand and his colleagues in Scandinavia, and by Harger,
Forney and their colleagues in the U.S.A., it appears that the mean
weight/volume blood/breath ratio at the temperature of the
expired air is 2,100/1—that is, one volume of blood at this
temperature contains the same weight of alcohol in solution as
is present as vapour in 2,100 volumes of breath. The blood-
alcohol concentration is then simply the breath-alcohol concentration multiplied by 2,100.

The actual methods used for the analysis of breath will be discussed in Chapter 6. Breath analysis is extensively used in this
way in many parts of North America, where blood-alcohol concentrations are used as corroborative evidence in proving impairment. However, it is not in practice as accurate a means of
determining blood levels as the above simple theory might suggest,
and for this reason it is not sufficiently reliable as a method of
analysis (as distinct from a simple screening test) when proof that
the blood-alcohol concentration exceeds a certain prescribed limit
is sufficient to secure a conviction without its being necessary or
relevant to show that driving was impaired.

Recent legislation in Northern Ireland, where a fixed-level
offence similar to that in Great Britain has been created, has also
made provision for breath analysis in enforcing this. The arrested
driver is given the option of accepting the result of a Alcotest
analysis (see p. 77) and a more accurate blood analysis is made only
if he asks for it.

Even in those published tests the results of which are most

favourable to the reliability of blood-alcohol determination via breath analysis (see e.g. *Harger, Forney & Baker* 1956; *Begg, Hill & Nickolls* 1962; *Fox et al.* 1965) the accuracy and reproducibility of the results were less, and the chances of an erroneous result greater, than could be considered acceptable for this purpose. Other researchers have been unable to achieve as good a correlation as was reported by those mentioned above between direct blood-alcohol analyses and determinations via breath analysis (see e.g. *Payne et al.* 1966) and the less-than-complete reliability of breath analysis was borne out by unpublished researches made during the drafting of the Road Safety Act 1967.

Indeed, the present practice in this country in operating the Road Safety Act 1967 is for breath-alcohol determinations to be used *only* as screening tests, and for their results not to be given in evidence, since the Act lays down that an offence can be proved only by laboratory tests made on blood or urine specimens.

In particular, in many cases measurement of blood alcohol by breath analysis has been found to give consistently low results at high blood-alcohol concentrations, the deficiency increasing with the concentration. There have also been numerous reports that the 2,100/1 blood/breath ratio is not as constant as has been assumed, or as would be necessary for breath analysis to be sufficiently reliable (See e.g. *Enticknap & Wright* 1965.)

One source of error is the fact that the assumed blood/breath ratio applies only to air *in equilibrium* with the blood—that is, air actually in contact with the walls of the alveoli—and not to the so-called tidal air, which is air merely breathed in and out of the respiratory passages. Breath-alcohol analysis *must*, therefore, if its results are to be significant, be made on specimens from which the tidal air has been excluded or eliminated. It is not easy to ensure this in practice. Some of the best experimental results are in fact based on the use of re-breathed air—that is, the same air breathed in and out more than once to ensure the attainment of equilibrium—a refinement of technique clearly impracticable in routine law-enforcement.

Another cause of possible error, which has been fully discussed by *Dubowski* (1962), is that the temperature of the expired breath may vary by several °C and that the precise blood/breath ratio is very temperature-dependent. (The variation is given as 5 per cent. per degree by Payne and as $6\frac{1}{2}$ per cent. per degree by Dubowski.) The 2,100/1 ratio is based on an assumed expired-air temperature of 34°C, but actual temperatures from 31° to 35° have been quoted, and the temperature has sometimes been found to rise by several degrees during the course of a single expiration.

However, in spite of all these objections, breath-alcohol analysis because of its speed and simplicity still constitutes a valuable and supremely convenient *approximate* method of measuring blood-alcohol levels.

Two other points that should be mentioned in connection with breath analysis are:

1. Since even the weakest alcoholic drink contains vastly more alcohol than is ever present in blood (*cf.* p. 10), the alcohol from any traces of drink remaining in the mouth would completely vitiate the results of an analysis made on breath blown out through the mouth. The time required for alcohol to disappear completely from the mouth depends slightly on the alcoholic strength of the drink consumed, but for practical purposes a time of 20 minutes can be assumed adequate for any drink. (See *e.g. Lins & Raudonat* 1962.) It has however been suggested that, exceptionally, traces of alcohol may linger longer than this behind dental plates or in unfilled tooth cavities.

2. Breath analysis has nothing to do with the smell of "alcohol" on the breath after drinking. The smell is in fact not due to ethanol (ethyl alcohol) at all, but to the various other volatile compounds ("congeners") present in practically all drinks and giving them their characteristic flavours and bouquets. (This is the origin of the belief in vodka leaving a "clean" breath; vodka is practically pure alcohol in water without congeners.) The smell may in fact persist after all alcohol has been eliminated from the body. In the same connection, it has been shown by numerous trials that the odorous substances present in bad or garlic-laden breath will not react as false "alcohol" in the methods used in breath analysis.

CHAPTER 4

EFFECTS OF ALCOHOL

THE grosser effects of alcohol are too familiar to need description. However, contrary to a popularly held belief, it is not a stimulant: it is a depressant or narcotic. Its apparently stimulating effects are due to the fact that it acts first on the so-called "higher" centres of the brain which govern the inhibitions, so that a loosening of the check which these exercise makes the drinker more responsive to the stimulation of the company and circumstances in which social drinking is usually done. In addition, its slight anaesthetic effect may make him less aware of depression or fatigue.

For the average occasional or moderate drinker, the correspondence between blood-alcohol levels and effects is, *very* approximately:

Blood Alcohol milligrammes/100 millilitres	Effects
Under 50	No obvious effect, except perhaps a tendency to talkativeness and a subjective feeling of well-being.
50–100	First obvious effects begin to appear: slurred speech, bravado, some loss of co-ordination and of sensory perception.
100–150	More marked loss of co-ordination, hence erratic or staggering gait; poor sensory perception; possibly nausea and/or a desire to lie down.
150–200	Drunkenness and probably acute nausea.
200–300	Probably coma ("passing out").
Over 300	Approaching the danger limit.
Over 450–500	Probably fatal (respiratory paralysis).

It must however be remembered that (1) persons, especially young persons, unused to drink will almost certainly show that succession of effects at lower blood-alcohol levels, and may well be markedly affected at levels below 100 or even below 50; (2) persons well habituated to drink will, correspondingly, show much less effect at any given level. In particular, real "soaks" and even more true alcoholics may show few outward effects at blood-alcohol levels at which the occasional drinker would be comatose, and there have been cases recorded of alcoholics appearing passably sober with levels around 300 milligrammes/100 millilitres.

It has been suggested, probably correctly, that normal social drinking rarely leads to blood-alcohol levels above about 50 milligrammes/100 millilitres. (See *e.g. Wright* 1963.) At the other extreme, most of the recorded fatal cases have shown figures in the 350-500 milligrammes/100 millilitres range. A reliably established figure below 350 probably indicates either some complicating factor (such as heart disease) or a delayed death from secondary effects (giving time for some elimination to have occurred), while a figure above 500 is sufficiently rare to be a matter of comment.

Broadly speaking, the effects of alcohol on driving performance can be studied in five ways.

1. By reasoning from the effects on other operations requiring attentiveness and good co-ordination.

2. By studying actual cases of alcohol-impaired driving, and correlating the observed behaviour with the results of subsequent examination and the blood-alcohol levels (if determined).

3. By arranging actual vehicle-handling tests in safe conditions, and correlating performance with blood-alcohol levels and/or amounts of drink consumed.

4. By tests in vehicle simulators, and correlating performance as in (3).

5. By a statistical study of the correlation between blood-alcohol levels and the incidence of accidents.

The third and fourth of these modes of testing have the advantage compared with the fifth that the experimental conditions can be accurately standardised and controlled, but the disadvantage that the subjects know that they are being tested and may not therefore behave as they would in actual driving.

EFFECTS IN GENERAL

A great deal of research has been done in this field, often by psychologists, and some of its results are clearly and directly applicable to driving performance. Research up to about 1955 has been admirably summarised by *Elbel & Schleyer*, pp. 133–160, from which many of the following details are taken. *Drew et al.* (1959) also give a short résumé of the subject on pp. 6–14 of their report.

It is clearly impossible to formulate any precise scale of measurement of the well-known effects of alcohol on *personality and behaviour*—the loud, babbling speech; the restlessness; the idiotic pranks; the irresponsibility; the loss of self-control. It is equally clear however that the appearance of just these last effects, in however small a degree, will transform a safe driver into a dangerous one. To quote *Elbel and Schleyer* (p. 133): ". . . they are probably a great deal more important as determinants of driving skill than any measurable impairment of mental capacity; in traffic they lead to situations in which the secondary effects of diminished sensory discrimination and precision of reaction become relevant, in that they weaken the driver's control of the situation. In short, the bad effect of alcohol on a driver is primarily conceptual rather than perceptual." Or, to quote *Loomis & West* (1958), "the severely intoxicated person is not the main public hazard as an automobile driver, but rather the person in a moderate state of intoxication who is not capable of reacting to an emergency situation with his normal efficiency."

Equally important is the drinker's diminished faculty for self-criticism and diminished ability to evaluate his own performance. In any sort of test requiring precise performance, keen perception and good co-ordination, it is quite usual for a test subject who has had some drink to think he is doing better than normal, when in fact he is doing worse. This effect, transferred to the road, means that the averagely competent driver is apt sooner or later to find himself in an accident-generating situation from which he might or might not be able to extricate himself if he was completely sober, but—even more important—into which he would never have got in the first place if he had not been affected by drink.

There have been several studies of the effect of alcohol on the capacity to sustain attentiveness—a capacity of obvious importance in modern traffic conditions. The results of these agree to the extent that impairment may be detected at blood-alcohol levels above 30-50 milligrammes/100 millilitres and that thereafter the capacity deteriorates steadily.

There have also been numerous tests of what may broadly be

called *dexterity*—the capacity to perform some simple mechanical task. Such tests will evaluate simultaneously co-ordination and proneness to fatigue, and the "score" is based on the time required to perform the task and/or on the number of mistakes made. In such tests, with blood-alcohol levels in the range 70-150 milligrammes/100 millilitres, the times required may be markedly increased and the number of mistakes made increased by several hundred per cent.

Sensory perception

Sight, hearing and touch have also been subjected to numerous tests, measuring both absolute sensitivity (that is, the threshold of perception) and sensitivity to small changes in the stimulus. In general, perceptible impairment at quite moderate blood-alcohol levels has been found. In the case of vision, general acuity, extent of vision, depth perception, accommodation (*i.e.* continuing ability to see after a sudden change from light to dark or vice versa) and resistance to dazzle or glare are all impaired, and the visual field is laterally reduced ("tunnel vision"). Moreover, it is pointed out by *Drew et al.* that "subjects are normally unaware of these changes in visual efficiency".

Another effect on the eyes, though not specifically on vision, is the phenomenon of lateral nystagmus—a side-to-side involuntary movement of the eyes. This may of course occur from several causes, but medical opinion seems to be almost unanimous that it is of all clinical symptoms one of the most reliable as an index that alcohol has been consumed.

Finally, among general effects to be mentioned is that on the reaction time. This seems to have caught the popular imagination, and is commonly the first if not the only effect to be mentioned in casual discussion of drink and driving. In fact, of all the faculties affected by alcohol, reaction times are possibly the most complex and therefore show the most ambiguous results when they are measured. For example, *Elbel and Schleyer*, the German authorities, say that "reaction times are less affected by alcohol than any other parameter measured in psycho-technical measurements" (*Elbel & Schleyer*, p. 152), while on the other hand *Rentoul, Smith and Beavers* (1962), of whom Dr. Rentoul is a very experienced Glasgow police surgeon, say: "There is no doubt that prolongation of visual motor reaction time is the most constant detectable sign of physical deterioration caused by alcohol."

The term "reaction time" is in fact ambiguous. Reaction times may be measured on either (1) pure reflexes (such as the knee jerk), which do not involve the higher centres of the brain, or (2) reactions requiring judgment or decision.

It would seem in fact to have been established that: pure reflexes ((1) above) may be slightly speeded up by small doses of alcohol, which can be accounted for by a reduced control of the lower nervous centres by the higher inhibitory ones; with more complex reactions, though there is some not very conclusive evidence of a slight speeding up immediately after a *small* dose of alcohol, the main effect is quite certainly a considerable increase in reaction time—increases ranging from 10 to 150 per cent. have been recorded for a range of blood-alcohol levels up to 150 milligrammes/100 millilitres. Although every independent investigator has found reaction time to increase with increasing blood-alcohol levels, no simple correlation between percentage increase and level can be detected. This is hardly unexpected, since different investigators used quite different types of measuring equipment, measuring reactions of different degrees of complexity.

As Elbel and Schleyer point out, it is the most complex reactions which are most relevant to actual traffic situations, where quick decisions between different possible courses of action may have to be made, and it does seem possible to draw the tentative conclusion from the figures they quote that, the more complex the reaction measured, the greater the increase in time required after a given dose of alcohol. They also state, quoting some earlier workers, that a very short interval between successive stimuli delays the response to each stimulus, which is very relevant to driving fast or in heavy traffic.

Effects: some additional points

Three other matters relating to the effects of alcohol in general which should be mentioned are: (1) the phase of the blood-alcohol curve; (2) habituation; (3) the personality of the drinker.

(1) There is some not altogether conclusive evidence that a given blood-alcohol level produces more effect during the rising than during the falling phase of the curve—that is, there appears to be a sort of "micro-habituation", so that the drinker can to some extent adapt himself to the effects of the alcohol while it is still circulating in his system. The earlier work on this point is

summarised by *Harger* (1962); see also *Gerchow & Sachs* (1961) and *Dennemark* (1963). See also p. 48.

(2) It is a well-known fact which need not be elaborated here that alcohol considered as a drug is habit-forming in the sense that persons used to taking it can take more without undesirable effects than can persons not so used. Without examining in detail the possible causes for this, it could be due either to a reduction in the concentration of alcohol reaching the brain, or to increased tolerance by the brain and central nervous system generally of a high cellular alcohol level, or to both these factors.

The effect of habituation on the blood-alcohol concentration has been extensively investigated experimentally, and many quite unjustified general conclusions have been drawn from inadequate or unreliable data. There have been reports of habituation speeding up absorption, slowing down absorption, producing a lower peak and producing a higher peak.

The most reliable earlier work produced, in most cases, no evidence of a greater rate of elimination in persons habituated to alcohol (see *e.g. Lester* 1965). However, recent investigations by *Bonnichsen* (1968), an authority who must be respected, have produced evidence of a significantly greater rate of elimination in alcoholics. The explanation for the apparent discrepancy may be that Bonnichsen worked with alcoholics who were bad enough to be hospitalised for treatment—a class of person probably not available to most of the earlier workers. One may perhaps tentatively conclude that habituation tends to produce some increase in the rate of elimination of alcohol, but that unless it reaches the stage of actual alcoholism this effect is so small as to be masked by normal personal variability.

In fact, following the extremely reliable and authoritative work of *Goldberg* (1951), habituation can be ascribed almost entirely to the second factor mentioned above—greater tolerance by the brain and central nervous system. Goldberg also points out, however, that, as habituated drinkers tend to drink more, the known slightly greater rate of elimination at very high blood-alcohol levels (*cf.* pp. 18-19) might also have some slight contributory effect.

(3) There have been a number of observations that the effects of alcohol vary according to the psychological type of the drinker. Most of these are of little significance in the present context, but it is of some interest that Drew (himself a professor of psychology) in his 1959 report (see p. 50 below) confirms earlier observations

that extroverts and introverts react in different ways to alcohol: in general extroverts tended in his experiments to drive after taking alcohol a little faster and much more erratically—to show a "couldn't-care-less" reaction—whereas introverts seemed to be anxious to demonstrate their unimpaired capabilities, by driving either faster (and usually rather worse) or with exaggerated caution. (Some of the drivers tested by Coldwell *et al.*—see p. 47—also behaved in this last way when under the influence of alcohol.)

THE CLINICAL EXAMINATION AND BEHAVIOUR OF ALCOHOL-IMPAIRED DRIVERS

Much useful information has been gathered, though often in a rather unsystematic manner, from the correlation of the results of clinical examinations and subsequently measured blood-alcohol levels. It may however be dismissed briefly here, since this sort of approach to the problem has now been overtaken by more recent and more systematic investigations.

Before the Road Safety Act 1967, there was no statutory obligation to call in a doctor at all, and some police forces did not at one time normally do so. However, because of the various illnesses and effects of injury which might, because of the similar symptoms produced, be mistaken for alcoholic intoxication, the prudent practice arose, and gradually became the norm, of calling in a doctor (often the local police surgeon) to examine the accused in order to discover whether there was any cause other than drinking which would account for the peculiar behaviour and/or impaired driving of the arrested person. (See also pp. 114-115 and 126-127.)

For the prescribed-level offence of the Road Safety Act 1967, since there is no need to prove impairment, a clinical examination is unnecessary. However, one will undoubtedly be made by the doctor called to take the blood specimen if it seems to him that the condition of the accused warrants it.

A full scheme for the medical examination of arrested drivers has been prepared by the British Medical Association, and is given on pp. 18-25 of *The Drinking Driver* (B.M.A., 1965). Readers are therefore referred to that publication for information about the purely clinical effects of alcohol discoverable by a medical examination.

Several attempts were made in the 1930's to correlate the results of medical examination with blood-alcohol levels. The results of these showed a fair degree of agreement that acute intoxication (*i.e.* obvious drunkenness) would be produced in many persons by blood-alcohol levels in the range 75-150 milligrammes/100 millilitres, and in all persons by levels above 150-180. (*Cf.* the table at the beginning of this chapter.) The last figure was generally quoted in most of the textbooks of forensic medicine as being that above which intoxication might be taken as certain.

It gradually became apparent, however, necessary though a clinical examination might be to detect injury or disease, that it was inadequate as a means of detecting a degree of intoxication short of drunkenness but sufficient to constitute a driving hazard. A committee of the American Medical Association appointed in 1936 reported in 1937 that ". . . 0·15 per cent. or more of alcohol by weight* in body fluids is associated with mental and/or physical inferiority . . . [and] much lower levels of alcohol are associated with definite impairment of judgment and particularly of self-criticism."

Later, the British Medical Association said (*Relation of Alcohol to Road Accidents* 1960, p. 33): "Relatively low concentrations of alcohol in the tissues cause a deterioraton in driving performances and increase appreciably the likelihood of accident," and "Clinical examination in the absence of biochemical tests is neither sufficiently sensitive nor reliable enough to detect deterioration in performance of his degree." (See also p. 115.)

It may therefore be of interest to note at this point that in this country during the 1950's the *average* blood-alcohol level of motorists charged with driving under the influence of drink was about 220 milligrammes/100 millilitres (approaching half the fatal level!—see p. 39) and that only about 10 per cent. of all drivers charged had levels under 150. (*Walls* 1958; *Haisman et al.* 1963.) Similar figures have been recorded in several other countries. (See *e.g.* the Californian figures given by *Bradford* 1966.)

Vehicle-Handling Tests

Tests of this kind have the advantage of requiring the minimum of special equipment, and several were carried out in both Ger-

---

* That is, assuming that this means per cent weight/weight, 150 milligrammes/100 grammes. Since the specific gravity of blood is about 1·06, this is equivalent to 150 milligrammes/94 millilitres or 159 milligrammes/100 millilitres.

many and the U.S.A. from the early 1930's onwards. These however have been superseded by later and more carefully designed tests of the same type.

The classic experiment of this type was the Swedish one reported by *Bjerver & Goldberg* in 1950. They were particularly concerned to test the effects of fairly low blood-alcohol levels, since by that time it was well recognised (at least in Sweden) that levels above about 100 milligrammes/100 millilitres seriously impaired driving ability. A team of thirty-seven skilled drivers took part; they were divided into two series, one to test the effect of beer and the other the effect of spirits, and each series was again subdivided into drinking and non-drinking (control) groups. Everything was carefully arranged so that any differences between the performances of the drinking and non-drinking groups would not be biased by fatigue, inherent differences in driving skill, etc.

The tests consisted essentially of relatively simple starting, steering, reversing, turning and parking exercises. Each group made two complete runs, with about an hour in between, through all the tests, and immediately after the first run the drinking groups were given their alcohol. The blood-alcohol levels of the beer drinkers were 39 to 56 milligrammes/100 millilitres (mean 46); and of the spirits drinkers 16 to 74 milligrammes/100 millilitres (mean 49). Scoring was on the basis of the times required to perform each operation *correctly*.

Most of the control drivers did better, some markedly better, on their second runs, because of the practice gained in the first, and the mean improvement in the control scores was 20 per cent. The drinking drivers, on the other hand, performed on the average about as well in the second test as in the first, and their mean score was unchanged. This, because of the way the experiment was designed, could mean only that alcohol had impaired performance to roughly the same extent as practice would have improved it. The actual extents of impairment ranged from 3 to 72 per cent. (mean 28). Thus, the authors concluded, blood-alcohol levels between 40 and 50 milligrammes/100 millilitres demonstrably impair performance by 25-30 per cent. Some further experiments and calculations showed that the threshold level (that is, that below which no impairment is detectable) seemed to lie around 20-30 milligrammes/100 millilitres.

Some years later a similar and in some respects more ambitious experiment was carried out in Canada under the aegis of the

Royal Canadian Mounted Police. (*Coldwell et al.* 1958.) Fifty drivers were used, and were grouped into "light" (=occasional), "intermediate" (=moderate), and "heavy" drinkers, with average weekly consumptions equivalent to 5, 23 and 76 fluid ounces (140; 650; 2,150 millilitres), respectively, of whisky. Scoring was by a combination of times required for correct performance of the tests and numbers of errors recorded; during the later parts of the experiment observers also rode with, without talking to, the drivers and assessed their general car-handling skill. (Numbers of errors appeared to provide the best single criterion of the effects of alcohol, and car-handling as evaluated by skilled observers the most sensitive index of impairment.)

The drink given was whisky, diluted to taste, initially in the quantity of 2 fluid ounces (55 millilitres) for each 50 lb. (23 kilo-grammes) body weight. Almost all the blood-alcohol levels of the drivers during the test runs were between 40 and 160 milligrammes/ 100 millilitres, and in rather over half the cases they were between 60 and 100.

The results and conclusions were; 1 driver showed impaired skill with 36 milligrammes/100 millilitres; in 5 out of 7 drivers signs of impairment were detectable at 50; no driver was unim-paired at 150; half the drivers showed statistically significant impairment at 78; heavy drinkers showed less impairment than light at the same blood-alcohol levels, but 8 out of 10 showed impair-ment within the 51-120 range of levels.

In another Canadian experiment a few years later (*Taylor & Stephens* 1962) fewer drivers were used (nine in all) but the tests were rather more elaborate, and included actual driving round a road circuit of 1·6 miles marked out on a disused airfield. A surprise event was arranged by suddenly pulling a large multi-coloured ball into the paths of the cars; the drivers knew it would appear, but not when or where, and they were told they had to avoid it. Rather more emphasis was placed on the reports of the observers, who made comments under various headings and assessed driving performance on a points system. Blood-alcohol concentrations were measured with a Breathalyzer (see Chapter 6), with at least ten and usually over sixteen measurements per subject.

One subject showed impaired driving with only 10 milligrammes/ 100 millilitres alcohol in his blood, and obvious intoxication with only 40. For the other eight subjects, impairment was first detect-able at concentrations between 40 and 100, and intoxication between

80 and 160. An interesting observation was that, in more than half the subjects, the blood-alcohol level at which impairment was detectable was lower during the rising (absorption) phase of the blood-alcohol curve than during the falling (elimination) phase. (*Cf.* p. 43). The difference between these two "just-impaired" levels amounted to 20-30 milligrammes/100 millilitres.

Another, British, experiment of this type (*Cohen et al.* 1958) is of great interest because in it an attempt was made to test the effect of alcohol on the driver's willingness to take a risk rather than primarily on his driving ability. As we have already mentioned, this is undoubtedly one of the most dangerous effects, if not the most dangerous effect, of alcohol. The test subjects were experienced Manchester bus drivers, whose normal drinking habits ranged from total abstinence to 20-30 pints (11½-17 litres) of beer a week. (Few of them drank spirits regularly.) They were divided into three groups—a control, a group receiving 2, and a group receiving 6 fluid ounces (55-170 millilitres) of whisky. Each driver was first asked to indicate the narrowest gap (marked by a pair of light posts) through which he *thought* he could always drive his bus, then to indicate the width of gap at which he was willing actually to try, and finally to make the attempt.

It was found that the alcohol impaired the drivers' actual performance only slightly (as would be expected in these fairly small dosages) but made it measurably more hazardous.* This is borne out by the following mean figures for the three groups.

	Narrowest gap which drivers believed they could always get through.	Narrowest gap which drivers in fact got through.
Control group ...	8ft. 1½in.	8ft. 6½in.
2-oz. group ...	8ft. 1½in.	8ft. 7in.
6-oz. group ...	7ft. 10½in.	8ft. 7½in.

Three of the drivers who had had only the smaller dose were in fact willing to attempt a gap actually 14 inches narrower than their buses! Professor Cohen summarises his results by saying: "The effect of alcohol was not to make the drivers take more

---

* Professor Cohen distinguishes between "risk-taking," which is embarking on a task without being certain of its success, and "incurring hazard," which is embarking on a task in which the performer will not always be successful.

risk*—that is, to act at a lower level of subjective probability†
[which means to embark on a task with less certainty of success]
—but to assign the same subjective probability to a more difficult
task."

Professor Cohen's results have been criticised on several grounds
—for example, that he was not sufficiently careful to ensure that
the difference between the control and the drinking groups was
only in respect of the drink taken. One may also wish that he
had secured more detailed reliable information than he did about
the actual blood-alcohol levels of his drivers. Nevertheless, his
experiment was a noteworthy pioneer one, and his results stand
so far unchallenged.

DUMMY CAR AND TRACKING SIMULATOR TESTS

Several pioneering investigations of this type were made in both
America and Germany during the 1940's, but two much more
comprehensive and thorough ones were carried out in the late
1950's, one in Seattle (Washington, U.S.A.) and one in this country.
In the former (*Loomis & West* 1958), the test subject had to "stop"
and "start" a dummy car with the usual controls at "traffic lights"
and, by steering, to keep a model car centred on an irregularly
moving black strip (the "road"). Scoring was on the basis of the
recorded reaction times to the "traffic lights" and the time during
which the "car" was off the road.

The ten subjects were first given weekly practice runs until
their performance showed little further improvement. Test runs were
then made approximately 1, $2\frac{1}{2}$ and $4\frac{1}{2}$ hours after the initial
drinking, and a blood sample taken for analysis after each run.
A unique feature of these experiments was that, in addition to
the initial drink, further drink was given as "maintenance doses"
in order to maintain as far as possible a uniform blood-alcohol
level during the whole period of the test. During the drinking-test
periods the subjects had blood-alcohol levels ranging from 30 to
180 milligrammes/100 millilitres.

The aggregated result was: some impairment could be detected
at blood-alcohol levels of 30 milligrammes/100 millilitres; on the

---

* See footnote on p. 48
† "Subjective probability" is the gambler's estimate of the, as opposed to
the true, chance of an event occurring.

average, performance had decreased to 85 per cent. of the control figure at blood-alcohol levels of 100 and to 70 per cent. of the control at 150. An interesting point was that performance fell off exponentially with increasing blood alcohol (*cf.* p. 61).

The subjects were also asked to fill in a questionnaire about how they *thought* the alcohol had affected their driving. Although all of them admitted being aware of having taken alcohol, sizeable minorities believed that their driving performances had actually improved during the last two hours.

The British investigation, which was carried out under the aegis of the Medical Research Council by a team headed by Professor G. C. Drew (a psychologist), was by far the most elaborate and exhaustive of this kind that has been done. (*Drew et al.* 1959.) It was specifically directed towards discovering the effect of quite small doses of alcohol. The subjects were given psychological personality tests as well as the actual "driving" ones. They had to "drive" along a winding country road projected on to a "windscreen". A most elaborate scoring system was devised, which took into account speed, driving errors and numbers of movements of the various controls. Each test lasted two hours—a period sufficient to ensure that subjects affected by alcohol could not "pull themselves together" for long enough to compensate for this effect in their performance.

There were forty subjects, thirty-five men and five women, and each was given alcohol in doses of 0·20, 0·35, 0·50 and 0·65 gramme per kilogramme of body weight. Similarly flavoured placebo drinks containing no alcohol were also given, so that the subjects did not know at the time of drinking whether they were taking alcohol or not. Each subject was tested after each dose and after the placebo—five tests per subject in all. This enabled each subject to be used as his/her own control. The *order* in which the tests were given was so arranged that: (1) it eliminated the effect on the results of any improvement due to practice; (2) as each order of tests was done by eight subjects, individual differences between the subjects within each group of eight could be fairly assessed. In one of the five-fold replications all of the five women subjects were used, in order to detect any sex differences. (None was found.)

Drinking lasted 10 minutes, and after a further 10 minutes the test began. Blood, urine and in some cases breath samples were taken during the course of the tests at 30, 60, 90 and 120 minutes after the end of drinking, and in some cases further samples were obtained up to 6 hours after drinking. The peak blood-alcohol levels naturally varied widely from subject to subject, as did the times after the end of drinking at which they occurred. Within these wide variations, however, the approximate mean peak levels and times were: 0·20 gramme/kilogramme dose—25 milligrammes/100 millilitre and 33 minutes; 0·35 gramme/kilogramme dose—42 and 39 minutes; 0·50 gramme/kilogramme dose —64 and 41 minutes; 0·65 gramme/kilogramme dose—80 and 42 minutes. As would be expected from the considerations outlined on pp. 12-19, there was a slight tendency for peaks which occurred early to be also rather higher, and for women (who have more fat in their bodies) to have higher peaks than men for the same equivalent dose.

The results of the investigation were subjected to an exhaustive and elaborate analysis, which is described in full in the report (*Drew, loc cit.*) Very shortly, the following were the main findings. Five of the subjects actually improved at the lower blood-alcohol levels, in that they "drove" more slowly, more consistently and with fewer errors. Others who also drove more slowly made more errors. Taking the results as a whole, however, impairment was detectable at concentrations as low as 20-30 milligrammes/100 millilitres, and there was in fact no evidence of a threshold concentration below which there would be no effect. For a level of 80 milligrammes/100 millilitres, the mean deterioration in performance amounted to 12 per cent. The connection which was found between personality and behaviour under the influence of alcohol has already been mentioned (p. 43).

Following publication of the Drew report, a committee of the British Medical Association, after carefully considering all of the evidence then available, published the opinion (*Relation of Alcohol to Road Accidents*, 1960, p. 33), which was widely quoted at the time and which was in fact very similar to the earlier American opinion mentioned on p. 45, that: "a concentration of 50 milligrammes of alcohol in 100 millilitres of blood while driving a motor vehicle is the highest that can be accepted as entirely consistent with the safety of other road users. . . . The committee is impressed by the rapidity with which deterioration occurs at blood levels in excess of 100 milligrammes/100 millilitres. This is true even in the case of hardened drinkers and experienced drivers. The Committee cannot conceive of any circumstances in which it could be considered safe for a person to drive a motor vehicle on the public roads with an amount of alcohol in the blood greater than 150 milligrammes/100 millilitres." It is of interest to compare that recommendation with the blood-alcohol levels found before the passing of the Road Safety Act 1967 in motorists charged with driving under the influence of drink (p. 45).

BLOOD-ALCOHOL LEVELS AND ACCIDENT STATISTICS

The numerous investigations which can be classified under this heading range from what are little more than informed casual observations to painstaking and elaborate statistical analyses, and it is impossible here even to enumerate them all.

It had become obvious to informed observers many years ago that in nearly every country of the world whatever official statistics were available grossly under-estimated the part played by alcohol in causing accidents. There was however an obvious need for studies of the problem in which the element of guess-work, however well-informed, was eliminated as far as possible. Such studies, made in various countries, all showed in various ways an obvious correlation between drinking and accidents. In this country, for example, it could scarcely be mere coincidence that on Saturday nights, while the traffic flow between 10 p.m. and midnight was just over half that during the mid-day and afternoon hours, the number of accidents rose suddenly and sharply after 10 p.m. to approximately double the mid-day figure. (See *e.g. Collister* 1962; *Jeffcoate* 1958; *Spriggs* 1958.) (See also p. 114.)

There can be no doubt, however, that the most useful and the most conclusive approach to the problem is one based on a correlation of the incidence of accidents with blood-alcohol levels of drivers. The pioneer study of this type was that carried out by *Holcomb* in Illinois and published in 1938. He measured the blood-alcohol levels of 270 accident casualties and those of a random sample during one week of 1,750 non-accident drivers, and compared the numbers of safe and accident-involved drivers at different levels. He found that drivers with no alcohol in their blood formed 53·4 per cent. of the accident group and 97·9 per cent. of the non-accident group. The ratio of these two figures, namely 53·4:87·9 is 0·6. The corresponding ratios for various ranges of blood-alcohol levels were:

Blood Alcohol (milligrammes / 100 millilitres)	Ratio
0— 60	1·9
70—100	3·3
110—140	8·7
Over 150	33·1

Although Holcomb's results have been criticised in that he was not sufficiently careful to ensure that his accident and non-accident groups were selected from exactly comparable traffic conditions, the inference to be drawn is inescapable.

No further investigation of this type was undertaken until after the war. Then S*mith & Popham* reported (1951) an investigation in Toronto in which, from the case histories of a large number of accidents, they were able to find 582 in which the victim was quite clearly either to blame or not to blame. Comparing the "responsible" and the "blameless" groups, they found that the proportion of those having blood-alcohol levels over 50 milligrammes/100 millilitres was eight times greater in the former than in the latter. (*Cf.* the results of the Grand Rapids Survey below.)

A later investigation, also from Toronto (*Lucas et al.* 1955), was carried out along the same lines as Holcomb's but with the additional precaution that the control (non-accident) group consisted of drivers passing the scene of each accident in cars of the same type and at about the same time of day. They obtained the following ratios (calculated in the same manner as Holcomb's):

Blood Alcohol (milligrammes / 100 millilitres)	Ratio
0— 50	0·85
50—100	1·31
100—150	2·10
Over 150	8·10

Similar results were obtained from an investigation in Czechoslovakia (*Vamosi* 1960). Surveys carried out in the 1950's in New York State, Baltimore City and Perth (Western Australia) of blood-alcohol levels in fatal accidents also showed that in all cases a large proportion of these (of the order of one half) were associated with high levels.

These investigations have however been dealt with briefly. The most exhaustive investigation of this type yet performed was the survey made in Grand Rapids (Michigan) in the early 1960's (*Borkenstein et al.* 1964), which is in a class by itself in respect of thorough and detailed preliminary planning and of the care and statistical sophistication used in the evaluation of the results. It was carefully considered in the White Paper, Road Safety Legislation 1965–66 (Cmnd. 2859), which stated specifically that there was no reason to suppose that at a given blood-alcohol level the performance of British drivers would be affected differently from that of American drivers. There can thus be little doubt that the survey's results had considerable influence on the drafting of the Road Safety Act 1967.

The primary purpose of the investigation was, taking the four groups into which all drivers can be divided, namely:

(1) Non-drinking — not involved in accident
(2) Non-drinking — involved in accident
(3) Drinking   — not involved in accident
(4) Drinking   — involved in accident

to discover whether there was any significant difference between the incidence of accidents for the non-drinkers (classes (1) and (2)) and the drinkers (classes (3) and (4)), and whether the proportions of drinking drivers were significantly different in the accident group (classes (2) and (4)) and the control group (classes (1) and (3)). In addition, however, a great deal of other valuable information was elicited.

Grand Rapids is a city in the peninsula between Lakes Michigan and Huron. A study of over three years' police records of where accidents occurred most frequently made possible the selection of a control group (classes (1) and (3) above) who were exposed to the same probability of accident involvement as drivers who had in fact been involved in accidents. The drivers who were stopped at random as controls were picked out by methods eliminating most rigidly any personal or other bias in their selection. In the event, during the 12 months in which the investigation was in progress, data were collected on 5,895 drivers involved in accidents, and 7,590 drivers not involved.

As it was extremely important to collect these data in such a way that the effects, if any, due to alcohol could be distinguished from those due to other driver variables such as sex, age, driving experience and so forth, a comprehensive questionnaire was designed. As far as possible, the following information was collected in every case: the details of the accident, if one had occurred; age; sex; estimated annual mileage; type of education; race or nationality; marital status; occupational status; details of the journey; frequency of drinking; where drinking is preferred; type of liquor preferred; when the last drink was taken; blood-alcohol levels as measured by breath analysis. (The breath samples were taken in blow-up plastic bags, which were taken back to the laboratory for the alcohol contents to be measured with a Breathalyzer.) The forms used also contained an entry for the interviewer's assessment of the truth of the answers given. To overcome as far as possible the expected and not unnatural reluctance of drivers to answer probing personal questions, the interviewers were specially trained in the methods used by the investigators who collected the data for the Kinsey reports on American sex habits.

In the statistical evaluation of the results, much use was made of the χ^2 ("Chi-square") test. This is a mathematical test used by statisticians to discover whether, when two groups of numerical results of any sort have different mean values, this difference between the means represents a real difference between the groups, or is likely to have arisen by chance. In this case, no difference which was found was accepted as real unless the data on which it was based showed that the odds on its being so were at least 19 to 1.

The mass of data collected were considered under either *single-factor analysis* or *two-factor interactions*. To deal first with the former, the problem was to discover whether the two main groups of drivers (those involved in accidents and those not so involved, which we shall call here groups A and NA respectively) showed any significant differences in respect of their various noted characteristics, taken individually—blood-alcohol levels, age, sex, driving experience, etc. Unless the Chi-square test showed a significant difference, it was assumed that it was *purely* a matter of chance whether a driver was involved in an accident or not.

This analysis showed that differences in every single one of the factors examined had some effect on liability to accident, but that the blood-alcohol level was by a large margin the most important in this respect; next, a long way behind, came age, followed by driving experience, with sex last.

Since no single factor was uniquely connected with the occurrence of accidents, any given accident might have been the effect of several together, and some attempt was made to elucidate their respective contributions by the analysis of *two-factor interactions*. This could not be applied to every possible interaction, since, taking into account the number of arbitrary divisions used for each factor (*e.g.* various ranges of blood-alcohol levels, age groups, etc.), the number of combinations to be examined would require data from millions rather than thousands of drivers. It was however shown quite clearly that, *within* each class (age group, drivers with similar driving experience, etc.), where sufficient data were available for the analysis, there was a highly significant correlation between accident liability and high blood-alcohol levels.

What is perhaps for our present purpose the most important single result to emerge from this investigation may be given in the words of the report on it (*Borkenstein, loc cit.* p. 125): "The effect of alcohol on accident experience in this study, using the test described, became statistically detectable at the 0·08 per cent. alcohol level class." (0·08 per cent.=80 milligrammes/100 millilitres. The "test described" is the Chi-square test. "Statistically detectable" means that the odds on its being a real and not a chance difference were at least 19 to 1; it does *not* mean that any difference detected at a lower blood-alcohol level could not be real also.)

Drivers with high blood-alcohol levels appeared more frequently in the accident than in the non-accident groups, as follows:

Blood alcohol mg./100 ml.

50-100	—$1\frac{1}{2}$ times as frequently
100-150	— 4 „ „
over 150	—18 „ „

Figure 9 shows the relationship between various ranges of blood-alcohol levels and the incidence of accidents. In fig. 10 the same data are presented in another way—namely as a relationship between blood-alcohol levels and the probability of being involved in an accident.

3,305 of the A group were also clearly, on the facts, solely responsible for the accidents in which they were involved. Within this sub-group, the following relationships were found (*Cf.* the *Smith & Popham* experiment of 1951, mentioned above, p. 53.)

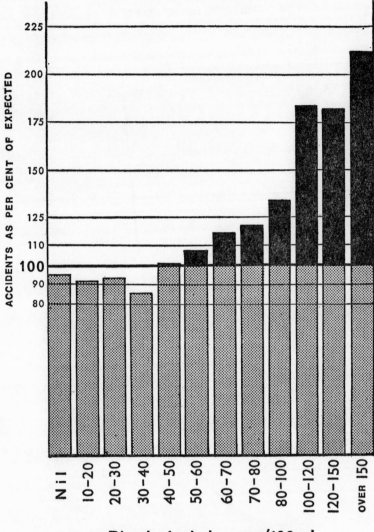

Fig. 9. BLOOD-ALCOHOL LEVELS AND ACCIDENTS—1
The data collected in the Grand Rapids survey can be assessed in several ways. One, which was used by the investigators themselves, is to compare the actual number of accidents occurring at each blood-alcohol level with the number that would have been expected within a group of that size *if there had been no connexion between alcohol and accidents*. That comparison is illustrated here. The actual number of accidents for each blood-alcohol level is shown as a percentage of the expected number. If the actual and expected numbers had been the same, each column would of course have reached exactly to the 100 per cent. line.

The "Nil" column includes all cases with blood alcohols below 10. The reduced incidence of accidents for blood-alcohol levels in the range 10-40 is discussed in the text.

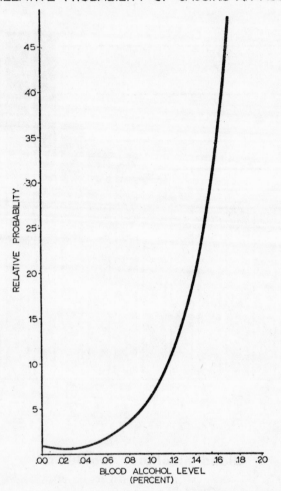

Fig. 10. BLOOD-ALCOHOL LEVELS AND ACCIDENTS—2

It is also possible to use the results of the Grand rapids survey to calculate the *probability* of an accident occurring at any given blood-alcohol level. (Note that ·10 per cent. blood alcohol corresponds to 100 mg./100 ml.)

Chart taken from *The Role of the Drinking Driver in Traffic Accidents* (report on the Grand Rapids survey).

Drivers with this level:

Blood-alcohol level	Formed following percentage of driving population (a)	Caused following percentage of accidents (b)	$\dfrac{b}{a}$
Positive (over 9mg./100ml.)	11	20	1·8
Over 50	3	15	5·0
Over 100	1	10	10.0
Over 150	0·15	6	40·0

It also emerged that there was a real tendency for drivers with high blood-alcohol levels to have more accidents in which no other moving vehicle was involved, and for their accidents to be more serious ones as measured by the damage and/or injury caused.

It appeared from a study of the two-factor interactions that, at the lower blood-alcohol levels, the proportions of group A drivers within each class (*i.e.* age group, length of driving experience, etc.) varied widely, but that with levels above 80 milligrammes/100 millilitres these differences tended to disappear. This result is of course not unexpected: as the blood-alcohol level increases, the relative importance of alcohol compared with the other accident-causing factors increases. To quote the words of the report (p. 169): "Apparently given sufficient alcohol, all drivers become about equally accident-involved."

There is one final point about the Grand Rapids investigation to be made. It appears from fig. 9 that there was a clear tendency for drivers with 10-40 milligrammes/100 millilitres of alcohol in their blood to be *less* involved in accidents than drivers with no alcohol at all in their blood. This prima facie rather surprising result not unnaturally attracted considerable attention when the report of the investigation was published. It can be interpreted in two ways:

(1) Drivers with these low blood-alcohol levels are in fact safer than drivers who have no alcohol in their blood.

(2) Some unconsidered and unsuspected factor was affecting the results.

Interpretation (1), while supported by the minute care with which the whole investigation was planned and conducted, is hardly consistent with the numerous reliable investigations, many of them mentioned earlier in this chapter, which have shown detectable impairment at these low blood-alcohol levels. If we accept interpretation (2), two explanations (which need not be mutually exclusive) have been advanced (together with the purely speculative suggestion that these classes contained a proportion of over-tired drivers who had stopped to relax over a drink, and to whom the rest did more good than the drink did harm).

(1) *Harger & Forney* (1967) have pointed out that in most cases the driver's blood-alcohol level would be falling during the period between the accident and the taking of the breath sample and that therefore the levels at the times of the accidents would be higher than those measured. On the assumption of a delay of 15 minutes and a consequent drop in the blood alcohol of 4 milligrammes/100 millilitres, the consequent revision of the figures would move many drivers into the next higher class of blood-alcohol levels. A recalculation of the results on this basis makes the ratio

$$\frac{\text{percentage of accident drivers}}{\text{percentage of control drivers}}$$

approximately 1 for all blood-alcohol levels of 40 and below—that is, makes drivers with blood-alcohol levels up and including 40 neither more nor less safe than completely sober ones.

(2) The explanation which is stated (*Goldberg & Havard* 1968) to have the support of the Grand Rapids investigators themselves is as follows. The alcohol-free group contained a large proportion of young inexperienced drivers who had a higher-than-average accident risk. The 20-40 milligrammes/100 millilitres range included a large number of middle-aged, well-to-do and experienced drivers who had a lower-than average accident risk which, even though it was increased by small doses of alcohol to a level above the average one for their group, remained lower than that of the driving population as a whole. The combined effect of these factors is to increase the accident-involvement index of the alcohol-free drivers and to decrease that of the 20-40 group of drivers.

It should also be noted that the blood-alcohol figures in the Grand Rapids survey were obtained by the analysis of breath samples taken in plastic bags. Experience in this country would tend to suggest that, if this led to any systematic error, it would be in the direction of giving low figures through loss of alcohol from the specimens. There is no evidence that this in fact happened, but if it did that would reinforce *Harger & Forney's* argument ((1) above).

Two final points

In all accident-statistics investigations the liability to accident increases much faster than do the blood-alcohol levels. The increase appears in fact to be approximately *exponential* (*cf.* fig. 10 and p. 50). *Ottis* (1963), using the results of the earlier investigations of this type, claims in fact to have shown (though *Freudenberg* 1964 does not altogether agree with him) that the relationship can be expressed mathematically by an exponential equation, and that this applies right down to zero blood-alcohol levels.

Lastly, it is very important not to confuse results from which predictions about the effects of alcohol on given individual drivers can be made, and results which predict only statistical probabilities. The Grand Rapids and similar investigations do *not* enable us to say that a particular driver must necessarily be impaired or more liable to accident with 80 milligrammes/100 millilitres of alcohol in his blood. Their results are therefore not inconsistent with the opinion of the British Medical Association quoted on p. 51.

CHAPTER 5

TAKING, PRESERVATION AND CARE OF SAMPLES

Note: In this and the following two chapters, *specimen* means the entire quantity of blood or urine submitted for analysis in one case, provided that it was all taken at substantially the same time, and *sample* means a portion of a specimen taken for analysis.

IF the results of an analysis are to have any value as evidence, it is clearly essential that the specimen analysed shall be identifiable beyond dispute and that it can be proved not to have been exposed to any possible source of contamination. It is also extremely desirable that it shall not lose any alcohol between taking and analysis and that nothing shall occur or shall be done to make its analysis more difficult.

Quite generally, a body fluid to be analysed may be (1) blood, (2) urine, (3) breath, or (4) some other fluid such as saliva. For obvious reasons, we shall be concerned here almost exclusively with (1) and (2). For completeness, we shall also discuss breath very briefly, but the case of any other fluid is too academic for consideration here.

BLOOD

Blood specimens submitted for analysis may be either (a) capillary blood taken from a skin puncture, or (b) venous blood taken by syringe. We have already seen (Chap. 3) that these, if taken from the same person at the same time during the absorption phase, may not show identical alcohol levels; the law, however, does not specify where or how the specimen shall be taken.

There is no doubt that it was originally envisaged that blood specimens taken under the Road Safety Act 1967 should normally be taken by skin puncture, on the assumption that the motoring public would accept this more readily than they would the taking of intravenous blood. Up to the time of writing, therefore, the blood-taking "kits" supplied to the police each consist of:

Four small plastic (polypropylene) cups with tight-fitting push-on lids and lugs for attaching identifying tags, and charged with sufficient anticoagulant/bacteriostat to keep the contents liquid and sterile. Each cup holds about one-third of a millilitre (several large drops). Three cups are to be used, the fourth being supplied as a spare in case one is lost or damaged;

four tags with spaces for entry of the relevant particulars identifying the specimen and wires for attachment to the cups by their lugs;

two stabbing lancets in sealed sterile packings;

two sterile dressing, also in sealed packings;

a tin for forwarding the specimen to the laboratory and bearing a label with spaces for entry of the relevant particulars identifying the case.

Before forwarding to the laboratory, the tin is sealed in the presence of the defendant with a suitable transparent adhesive tape in such a way that it can be opened without defacing the label *only* by cutting the tape, and that any attempt to remove the tape will deface the label.

The plastic cups were chosen after extensive tests from several alternative types of receptacle. None was without some disadvantage, but the cups proved to be on the whole the most suitable, taking into account: (1) ease of filling; (2) risk of loss of alcohol from the specimen; (3) manipulative convenience in analysis.

There is no statutory requirement that these kits shall be used, but if blood is sent for analysis packed in any other way the court may wish to satisfy itself that identity is proven and tampering or accidental contamination with alcohol impossible, and the analyst will expect the blood to be preserved from clotting and bacterial action.

The anticoagulant/bacteriostat in the cups is a mixture of a soluble fluoride and a soluble oxalate, in quantity sufficient for a cupful of blood. This mixture has been found to be the most effective preservative: the combination of salts prevents the blood from clotting and the fluoride, which is a powerful bacterial poison, inhibits the growth of bacteria which might change the alcoholic content of the specimen. These salts are at the time of writing put in by the forensic science laboratory supplying the cups to the police, and, being themselves colourless, they are usually coloured with a dye before putting in the cups, merely as aid to distinguishing prepared cups from empty ones during the packing operation in the laboratory.

There are, however, several serious disadvantages (see below) in the collection of capillary blood by skin puncture, and since the Road Safety Act 1967 came into force, the motoring public has apparently accepted more readily than was envisaged the taking of venous blood specimens by syringe. This latter is in fact fast becoming the normal method: it is now recommended by the Association of Police Surgeons of Great Britain, and it will eventually probably replace altogether blood collection by skin puncture. Many police forces therefore now provide for their doctors' use disposable sterile syringes and needles as well as the kits described above.

The collection of blood specimens

Whichever type of specimen is taken, the following procedure has been authoritatively recommended.

Written notes should be taken, preferably at the time. These should obviously include the day of the week, the date and the time of the doctor's arrival at the police station.

The doctor should allow himself to be introduced to the accused by the police officer. He should then ask the officer, in the presence and hearing of the accused, whether the accused has had the legal consequences of refusal to give a blood specimen (or two urine specimens) explained to him, and whether he appears to have understood them. That is, the doctor should satisfy himself that the accused understands that he may refuse to furnish a specimen of blood, or two specimens of urine, but that this refusal may itself be an offence (if the request is made under section 3 of the Road Safety Act 1967), or may be used as evidence against the accused (if the request is made under section 2 of the Road Traffic Act 1962). This having been done, the doctor should then ask the accused's permission to take the specimen.

Permission having been given in the hearing of the police officer, the accused should be conducted to the room set aside for the use of the police surgeon. He should there be seated comfortably at the side of a table and the equipment set out. He should be told the place from which the doctor proposes to take the specimen, whether the area of skin for capillary blood or vein for venous blood. (It is now established that the doctor has a professional discretion as to where the specimen is to be taken—see pp. 142-143.)

The doctor should wash his hands with soap and water in the presence of the accused, and dry them. He should then wash the region chosen for the taking of the blood specimen with plain soap, water and clean (preferably sterile) cotton wool, and dry it.

The collecting cups and their caps should be arranged for convenient handling, and their order of use in collecting the blood maintained. (Only three cups are required.)

The accused should be warned that the procedure—particularly if a capillary specimen is to be collected by "stabbing"—is not painless. This has been found psychologically a better form of words than saying something like "it may hurt a bit" (although the reaction to both the words used and the stab or insertion of the needle will probably be governed by the quantity of alcohol in the accused's blood).

The blood specimen should then be taken. (The various points which arise in ensuring that the specimen is adequate and fit for the subsequent analysis are discussed below—see pp. 68-72.)

The accused having been tidied up and the skin puncture covered with the adhesive dressing, in his presence the doctor should complete the wired labels, marking them 1, 2 and 3 respectively, and in the same order fasten them with the wires through the perforated lugs of the cups.

The labelled cups marked 1 and 3 should be replaced in the tin, the lid of this closed and the label on the lid completed, the police officer signing on the bottom line. The tin should then be sealed with Sellotape, so as to cover the label and ensure that the tin cannot be tampered with before its arrival at the laboratory. It should finally be replaced in its original envelope and handed to the police officer in the presence of the accused.

Cup no. 2 shsould be offered to the accused for him to have analysed independently if he wishes. The recommended procedure so far has been for the cup to be placed in a clean envelope, which is then sealed by its adhesive, after which the accused and the police officer sign across the closure. (See however p. 71, below.) The specimen should then be handed to the police officer for custody along with the other property of the accused, to whom it should be explained that he will receive the sealed specimen on his release and that he may have it independently analysed if he wishes. (See also p. 142.)

A note should be made of the time at which the whole procedure is finished.

(The above recommendations on procedure are based, by kind permission of the author, Dr. Charles H. Johnson, on Chapter 11 of *The Practical Police Surgeon.*) See also pp. 126-127.

If capillary blood is taken by skin puncture, it is important that it is allowed to drop directly from the incision into the cup, so that at least two and preferably three sizeable drops per cup are collected. Alcohol may be lost by evaporation if blood at skin temperature is exposed for too long as a hanging drop or is allowed to run over the skin as a film. Most police surgeons have their own adequate methods for ensuring a good flow of blood from an incision, but it is important that the digit punctured should not be "milked," since this may lead to the collection of a specimen with a greater plasma/cell ratio than the circulating blood. There has been some dispute about the ratio in which blood alcohol is distributed between the plasma and the cell contents (see *e.g. Payne et al.* 1968; Wright 1968—I), but, whatever the correct value for this, plasma certainly contains proportionately more alcohol than does the whole blood, so that a specimen containing more plasma than the circulating blood would lead to a falsely high figure on analysis. (This is however more of a theoretical than a practical difficulty. If it was so difficult to get enough blood that there was a temptation to "milk" the digit, then the blood would almost certainly be exposed to the air for so long during the process of collection that the net result would be a loss of alcohol, leading to too low rather than too high a figure.)

The advantages and disadvantages of the two methods of collecting blood specimens are, briefly.

Capillary blood by skin puncture
Advantages

(1) If there is any contamination of the skin, it will be more easily detected. (See below.)

Disadvantages

(1) Contamination of the specimen from the skin is inherently more probable.

(2) A stab deep enough to collect sufficient blood is decidedly painful.

(3) It may be difficult to get enough blood from *one* stab, especially in cold weather. (See below for the legal implication of this point.)

(4) There is a risk of getting a plasma-enriched specimen. (See above.)

(5) Alcohol may be lost in collecting the specimen. (See above.)

(6) There is some risk of the blood clotting during collection if this is protracted.

Venous blood taken by syringe

Advantages

(1) Contamination of the specimen from the skin is inherently less probable, since the blood does not come in contact with it during collection.

(2) It is almost painless if skilfully performed.

(3) There is no difficulty in securing an adequate specimen.

(4) There is no risk of getting a plasma-enriched specimen.

(5) There is no risk of the loss of alcohol by exposure of the blood to the air during collection.

(6) The risk of clotting is non-existent or at least minimal.

Disadvantages

(1) If there is any contamination from the skin, it may be more difficult to detect this.

There are some further points arising from the above comparison and also generally applicable to the taking of blood specimens by either means.

The Road Safety Act 1967 authorises the taking by a doctor with consent of the accused of *a* specimen of his blood. This must mean sufficient blood to enable the purposes of the Act to be carried out. The Act itself gives no guidance on quantity. It is arguable however, that the Act permits only one extraction, and the legality of a second "jab" or a second syringe, if the first through inexperience or lack of skill or foresight proved insufficient, is certainly open to question and has not yet been considered by the courts.

Most police surgeons recommend that the specimen should be divided into three parts one of which is used for the official analysis, another being made available to the accused. This is not directly enacted in the statutory provisions of the Road Traffic Act 1962,

s. 2, which merely provides that where the accused at the time of providing the specimen asks to be supplied with such a specimen, evidence of the analysis is not to be admissible unless the accused received either a part of the original specimen or a second specimen taken on the same occasion. The Act, however, goes on to require that the constable requesting a person to supply blood or urine specimens must offer to provide him with a specimen for his own use. In this way he is made aware of his right to request a part of the specimen.

The provisions of section 3 of the Road Safety Act 1967 under which the blood samples are required for laboratory testing in connection with the impairment offence are similar but make no provision for an offer by the police of a specimen for the defence, though this is obviously an excellent procedure to adopt.

Skin contamination

However the blood is taken, the skin will normally be cleaned before incision or venu-puncture. It is clearly essential that this shall not lead to contamination of the specimen by ethanol, and most desirable that no other volatile compound shall be used. Organic liquids such as ether or *iso*-propanol, sometimes used in other circumstances as skin sterilisants, may contain small amounts of ethanol, and should not therefore be used. Some proprietary antiseptic creams appear to be satisfactory in this respect. Clearly however soap and water is the safest from this point of view.

If contamination of the specimen from the skin *has* occurred, it should be detectable in the case of a capillary specimen through the concentration of contaminant in the specimen being highest in the first cup filled and lowest in the last. (That is why it is recommended that the prosecution should receive the first and last cups filled, so as to facilitate the detection of contamination by maximising the difference). The detection of contamination even in syringe specimens has been reported, different contaminant concentrations having been found in the separate cups. It must be assumed that in such cases complete mixing does not take place in the syringe, so that the first cup is filled with the last of the blood withdrawn, and vice versa. Obviously, however, one cannot depend on this occurring.

If the contaminant is ethanol, then, although the fact of contamination may be detected as just described, the results of the analysis will of course be worthless as evidence. If the contaminant is some other volatile compound, the presence of this in the specimen will not interfere with the detection and determination of ethanol by gas chromatography. However, before the result of the analysis could be used in evidence, *there would have to be a subsidiary analysis of the contaminating sterilisant to ensure that it contained no trace of ethanol* (an eventuality which would not be welcomed by a busy analyst!)

In the early days of the operation of the Road Safety Act 1967, quite large differences between the blood-ethanol concentrations in the different cups were sometimes encountered even when, in all the circumstances, including a statement of his procedure by the doctor who took the specimen, external contamination by ethanol could be confidently excluded. In such cases, the differences could always or almost always be ascribed to loss of alcohol from the blood in one of the cups, probably because of exposure to the air at skin temperature during filling (see above). When this occurs, the laboratory will report the lowest blood-alcohol figure found (although, for the reasons given above, the higher is probably more correct).

If specimens are collected in non-disposable syringes which require prior sterilisation, it is obviously essential that no alcohol, and highly desirable that no other volatile liquid (which may contain traces of alcohol), is used for this purpose. Common sense would seem to make this warning unnecessary, but cases have occurred which show that it is not.

When blood specimens, however collected, are transmitted in the plastic cups in current use, it is most important (1) to press the lid on *firmly*, and (2) to shake the cup thoroughly after doing so. Failure to perform (1) may result in loss of alcohol from the specimen and/or actual seepage of blood from the cup. If (2) is not done, the anticoagulant/bacteriostat will probably not be properly dissolved, and the blood will probably clot and may putrefy or decompose if not immediately refrigerated. Ensuring that the anticoagulant is dissolved is also important if an evacuated venule is used to take blood. Although clotting does not necessarily prevent an accurate analysis being made (a special "gadget" has been devised for breaking up clots in cups), it makes it more difficult and increases the risk of failure.

It has, however, been established that, properly handled, the cups in present use will preserve a specimen for *at least* a week under any reasonable conditions of storage.

Clotting

Much research has been devoted, especially in Germany, to discovering the relative alcohol concentrations in the clot and the
overlying serum when blood containing alcohol has clotted. (See
e.g. Elbel & Schleyer, p. 127, *Illchmann-Christ* 1959; *Hallermann
et al.* 1960; *Steigleder* 1961.) It would obviously be convenient if
the serum: clot or serum: whole blood alcohol ratios were known
and invariable, since a reliable figure for the blood could then be
very easily obtained by analysis of the supernatant serum. However, although the mean serum:clot ratio appears to be around 1·5,
and the mean serum: whole blood ratio around 1·2 (*cf.* the urine:
blood ratio), the figures are much too variable and uncertain
(depending as they must do on the red-cell content of the blood,
length of storage, density of clot and possibly other factors) to be
used in determining a legally critical whole-blood alcohol level.

Defence specimens

Present practice is to send two specimens of blood (preferably
the first and third, if they are taken separately—see above) for
analysis on behalf of the prosecution and to offer another for
analysis on behalf of the defence. This system seems on the whole
to work satisfactorily, in that (as far as the writers can discover)
it is the rule rather than the exception for competent independent
analysts for both sides to obtain concordant results. Difficulties
have however been encountered. There have been cases in which,
when there has been a failure to obtain three adequate specimens,
the specimen received by the defence analyst has been too small
for analysis. This clearly defeats the plain intention of section 3(5)
of the Road Safety Act 1967 that the defence should have the
opportunity of having an independent analysis made. It is therefore
most important to ensure that, if the defence is offered and accepts
a specimen, it is a proper and adequate one. (See also pp. 141-144.)

The present practice has also been criticised—and the criticisms
seem to be valid ones—on three grounds:

(1) it is not always understood by accused persons, and is
often apparently not explained to them, that the analysis
should be carried out within a few days and that with these small
quantities of blood only micro-methods of analysis are adequate.
This means in practice gas chromatography (see Chap. 6), the
equipment for which is not universally available. The Royal

Institute of Chemistry (30 Russell Square, London W.C.1.) has published a list of private analysts prepared to undertake this work. Some police forces offer informal guidance on these points. A better understanding of the procedures involved—which the authors of this book have tried to supply—may also help.

(2) The "sealing" of the specimens received by defence analysts has been quite inadequate, so that the analysts have been unable to testify under oath that they were satisfied that the samples could not have been tampered with. (See also p. 142.)

(3) Small plastic cups of blood should not be sent by post in unprotected envelopes, because modern mechanised Post Office sorting methods may involve passing the envelopes between rollers. Cases have occurred of specimens being received by analysts with the cups flattened and the contents lost.

There seems therefore to be a case for re-examining the methods used for the transmission of defence samples. Although the difficulty of securing sufficient blood from a skin puncture makes it unreasonable to suggest that the defence should also receive two cups of blood as long as this method of collection is in use, criticisms (2) and (3) would be met if the defence specimen(s) were, like the prosecution's, transmitted in some sort of sealed tin.

Storage and preservation of blood samples: further discussion

Although it can safely be assumed that a specimen of blood which has been properly treated (see above) will afford a true and accurate figure for the blood-alcohol concentration at the time at which it was taken, it is obviously desirable to know as much as possible about what may happen to the specimen in less-than-ideal conditions or on prolonged storage, and a great deal of research has been done on this topic. This has mainly been directed towards:

(1) the possibility of losing alcohol on prolonged or improper storage;

(2) the effects of inadequate preservation and bacterial contamination.

As far as (1) is concerned, it may safely be taken as a working rule that alcohol will be lost if the specimen is for any length of time (a) left unsealed, or (b) exposed to a high ambient temperature. "Any length of time" is admittedly, but unavoidably, a vague term; however, it should probably be measured in minutes rather than hours, and experienced analysts make a practice of never leaving their specimens unstoppered or unsealed for longer than necessary for the withdrawal of the quantity required for analysis. A "high" ambient temperature means, ideally, any temperature higher than that inside a refrigerator; in practice, however, it has been found that properly sealed or stoppered specimens may safely be stored for a considerable time at ordinary room temperatures.

A point sometimes raised is that a specimen may lose alcohol if it is in a container much too large for it. Whilst it is true that the container should not be larger than necessary and should be, say, at least one-third full, any loss which could occur in this way will be barely significant.

It is in short generally agreed that if a sterile specimen fills a reasonable proportion of its container, and if this is kept tightly stoppered in a cool or cold place, no significant loss of alcohol will occur in a time which is measured by weeks or even months. (*Elbel & Schleyer*, pp. 117-121.) It is a common experience in the forensic science laboratories, if they must for some reason re-analyse a specimen weeks after it was first analysed, to find that if it has been properly stored the alcohol content has dropped by only a few milligrammes/100 millilitres.

(2) If however the specimen is not sterile and bacteria are allowed to contaminate and grow in it, and if it is not adequately refrigerated, large changes in its alcohol content may be produced. This most commonly seems to take the form of a *loss* of alcohol, which, though undesirable, would not lead to injustice. (See *e.g. Elbel & Schleyer*, p. 119; *Krauland et al.* 1960; *Gehm & Schmid* 1962; *Schwerd et al.* 1967.) However, in some circumstances some types of bacterial contamination can lead to *production* of alcohol in quantities comparable with those sought in the present context. (See *Osterhaus & Johannsmeier* 1966; *Blackmore* 1968.) Clearly evidence based on the analysis of such a specimen would be worthless. If this has occurred, it would probably never be possible to say how much of any alcohol present was there originally and how much was produced by bacterial action; however, a bacteriological examination would settle the question whether any could have been produced by the latter means; in addition, bacterially produced alcohol is generally accompanied by certain other characteristic compounds which can be detected by gas chromatography (*Blackmore, loc. cit.*)

If fluoride is used as a bacteriostat, at least 1 per cent. must be present in the specimen for it to be effective (*Blackmore, loc. cit.*).

URINE

Urine specimens present fewer problems of preservation, storage and possible contamination. All that is normally required is that they shall have been taken in a clean container and transmitted in a sealed bottle containing enough of a suitable preservative. (A clean dry container is sometimes prescribed. This, though possibly desirable, is not important; if the container has been rinsed in clean water and drained, the dilution of a, say, 8-ounce (200-250 milli-litres) specimen of urine by the water adhering to the sides of the container will almost certainly be undetectable. If however the bottles to be used for transmission already contain the preservative, it is very important that they should *not* be rinsed.)

The preservation of urine specimens is important chiefly because, if they contain any sugar (as they may if taken from diabetics and in certain circumstances from healthy persons) then contamin-ation by stray yeast spores could otherwise lead to the production of alcohol by the fermentation of this sugar. The preservative most commonly recommended and used is phenyl mercuric nitrate; this is soluble to the extent of about 1 part in 1,000, and sufficient to ensure a saturated solution is added either by "pre-dosing" the bottles before they are issued to the police or as a tablet when the bottle is being filled.

In the analysis of urine specimens for alcohol, therefore, a number of subsidiary tests are always made. These may include: (1) a test for the presence of the preservative; if no preservative is present, then (2) sugar may be tested for, and (3) a further test is made to ensure that alcohol has not been, or is not being, produced by the fermentation of sugar by (a) centrifuging and searching the sediment microscopically for yeast cells, and/or (b) leaving the specimen for some days at room or incubator temperatures, fol-lowed by re-analysis to see whether the alcohol content has in-creased. Yeasts will not grow in properly preserved urine specimens, but if it is ever found that alcohol is in fact being produced by fermentation, then of course the evidential value of the specimen is nil.

Contamination of urine by bacteria (as opposed to yeasts) is unlikely to lead to the production of ethanol (*Blackmore, loc. cit.*).

BREATH

The analysis of breath for alcohol is normally done on the spot, but samples can be taken and transported in plastic bags for subsequent analysis. This was the method used in the Grand Rapids accidents survey (Chapter 4), and it has been extensively investigated in this country (see *Begg, Hill & Nickolls* 1962) and elsewhere.

Errors if any will arise from the loss of alcohol vapour, leading to too low results. This loss could occur because (1) of a defective seal, (2) the material of the bag adsorbs or is permeable by alcohol vapour, (3) the bag is not sufficiently warmed before its contents are expelled for analysis, so that alcohol is trapped in solution in condensed moisture.

In spite of the numerous reports of the successful use of such bags, experience in this country is that the analytical errors entailed by their use are too great to be tolerable in the enforcement of a fixed-level law.

IDENTITY AND INTEGRITY OF SPECIMENS

It is clearly essential that every possible precaution is taken to ensure that, in every case, the figure given by the analyst on his certificate or in evidence relates to the specimen taken from the defendant in the case.

This is the responsibility of the police officer(s) until the specimen reaches the laboratory, and it is normally discharged with exemplary correctness. It is not unknown, however, for different versions of the same name to appear on the specimen label and on the accompanying form, which, though a venial error, is undesirable.

Since the police officer usually deals with only one specimen at a time, whereas the analyst normally deals with a number every day, the latter has clearly the more onerous task in this respect. It is his responsibility to satisfy himself and to testify if necessary that he has not made a mistake in his figures or got his specimens muddled up. How he does this, being his responsibility, is his affair. Generally, however, it is very desirable to use a system which avoids the copying of results from one piece of paper to another, and as far as possible to write down the figures at the time once and for all on what will be the final document in the case. Most careful analysts also make a point of minimising the risk of confusion by having only one case on their bench at a time, and of clearing away the specimens in that case before bringing out those in the next. This procedure admittedly delays the analysis of a succession of specimens, because technically it would be easy to start each specimen whilst the previous one is being processed; in the circumstances, however, the delay is well justified and must be accepted.

With blood specimens, even if they were not sealed, the risk of a fraudulent substitution by another specimen containing less or no alcohol is small because of the practical difficulties involved; also, even if one could envisage circumstances in which it was in anyone's interest to increase the alcohol content of a specimen, to add a small enough amount of alcohol for the falsification not to be immediately apparent on analysis is for all practical purposes impossible.

With urine specimens, on the other hand, given the opportunity it is a simple matter to dilute an unsealed specimen with water or to replace it by alcohol-free urine. Supervision in the taking of the sample and its proper sealing are therefore important. For example, if a reputable and competent defence analyst reports a figure much lower than that found by the prosecution, and if it transpires that the defendant himself delivered an unsealed specimen to the analyst, the inference is obvious. At least one case is recorded of a defendent (who was also a magistrate), having professed extreme modesty and asked to be allowed to provide his specimen in privacy, offering a well-diluted specimen from the lavatory pan into which he had just urinated. Dilution with water may be detectable if analysis of the specimen for the constituents of urine (chiefly urea, salts and amino-acids) shows the amounts of these present to be below the lowest limits found in normal urine. However, such an analysis would not be made unless suspicion had been aroused. In any case, its results must be interpreted very cautiously, since urine passed after drinking is usually rather dilute owing to the diuretic effect of alcohol, so that the constituents mentioned may in any case be present in abnormally low concentrations. There is needless to say no chemical means of detecting the substitution of one specimen of urine for another.

As a footnote to this chapter, one of the present writers in the early days of these tests received for analysis a specimen of urine contained in a gin bottle bearing its original label. He had no reason to suppose that there had not been at least an honest attempt to wash out the bottle properly, but he could not help feeling that a more suitable container might have been found.

CHAPTER 6

ANALYSIS: METHODS

[See note at head of Chapter 5.]

QUITE different methods of analysis are necessary according to whether the specimen is a gaseous (breath) or a liquid one (blood or urine). We shall discuss the former first.

A. BREATH ANALYSIS

For an analysis of a breath specimen to be of any value in the present context, it must be performed on: (1) alveolar and not tidal air—*i.e.* air from the lungs and not air from the respiratory passages (*cf.* pp. 34-37); (2) a known volume of breath at an (at least approximately) known temperature. (Temperature is important because the volume of a gas is very dependent upon temperature.)

Most of the currently used methods of breath analysis determine alcohol vapour by allowing it to react with chromic acid or (which amounts to the same thing) a mixture of a bichromate with sulphuric acid. This reaction produces a colour change from orange or yellow to green. It is in fact a quite unspecific reaction and is given by practically any volatile reducing substance; alcohol is however the only such substance which occurs in any significant quantity in expired breath.

Breath analysis may be used as either a fairly accurate index of, or an approximate guide to, the blood-alcohol level (*cf.* Chap. 3); quite different types of apparatus are used for these two purposes.

Breath analysis: accurate methods

All types of equipment designed for this purpose incorporate some mechanical device for automatically measuring a fixed volume of expired breath at a fixed temperature. The problem of ensuring that the analysis relates to alveolar air has been met in two ways:

(1) (Now obsolete.) By measuring both the alcohol and the carbon dioxide content of the expired air. Since the carbon dioxide content of alveolar air is fairly constant, a calculation using both measurements gives the alcohol content of the alveolar air.

(2) By making some arrangement for automatically rejecting the first, say, 500 millilitres of the expired air and collecting for the alcohol determination only the last part of a deep expiration, which may be assumed to be alveolar air.

The currently best-known and most successful apparatus for accurate breath-alcohol analysis is the *Breathalyzer** designed by *Professor Borkenstein* of Indiana University. (For a description and evaluation see *Borkenstein* 1960; *Borkenstein & Smith* 1961; *Coldwell & Grant* 1963—I.) The actual analysis is made by allowing the alveolar air collected to bubble through the reagent contained in an ampoule, the extent of the colour change from yellow to green produced by alcohol being then accurately measured photo-electrically. This is a sophisticated (and fairly expensive) instrument, which is extensively used for blood-alcohol determinations by breath analysis in North America. It measures breath alcohol very accurately; as already explained, however, this does not necessarily measure blood alcohol with as high an accuracy.

In a somewhat similar, but rather simpler and cheaper, instrument designed some years ago by *Professor Kitagawa* (Yokohama) and *Dr. B. M. Wright* (London), the reagent, instead of being present as a solution in an ampoule, was carried on a column of inert solid granules. Alcohol concentration was measured by the length of column which changed from yellow to green. (See *Kitagawa & Wright* 1962; *Kitagawa* 1962; *Wright* 1962.) This instrument appears to be convenient and quite accurate, but it never (as far as the writers are aware) went into commercial production.

Breath analysis: approximate methods

Most of these, and certainly the most successful, depend (as with

---

* The registered name *Breathalyzer* refers specifically to this instrument. Is is unfortunate and misleading that the press always refer to the breath-testing device used here by the police (the *Alcotest*—see p. 78) as a "breathalyser."

the Kitagawa-Wright instrument mentioned above) for their action on the length over which a column of inert granules (silica gel) impregnated with the reagent (bichromate/sulphuric acid) changes colour when alcohol-laden breath is blown through it. No special provision is or can be made for collecting alveolar air only; instead, a fixed volume of breath is blown through the column and it is assumed that a sufficiently constant proportion of this is alveolar air. Because of this assumption (which cannot always be strictly correct), because the weight of breath collected probably varies slightly with the external temperature, and because the columns must be short (so that it is impossible to measure the length of colour change very accurately), devices of this type cannot be other than fairly rough guides to breath-alcohol concentration. The column is kept short because it would be difficult or even impossible to blow through a long one, and so that the whole device can be carried in a policeman's pocket.

The device of this type now used by the police in this country is a proprietary one known as the *Alcotest* (though the press always refer to it as the "breathalyzer"—see footnote on p. 77). With this, the suspected driver is asked to blow through the reagent column so as to inflate and fill an inelastic plastic bag, thereby delivering an approximately fixed volume of breath (about 1 litre). The reagent is contained in a glass tube bearing a mark on the outside at such a (fixed) distance from the beginning of the column that the colour change just reaches it when the breath-alcohol concentration corresponds to a blood-alcohol level of 80 milligrammes/100 millilitres. The tube as supplied is sealed at both ends, and immediately before use the sealed ends must be cut off for attachment of the plastic bag and a mouthpiece. (See also pp. 139-140 and 145.)

The Alcotest does not pretend to be a highly accurate means of measuring breath alcohol, and it does not seem possible to make it produce better than about 85-90 per cent. of correct results. (That figure is based on the numbers of drivers whose breath gives a positive Alcotest reading but whose blood-alcohol level turns out on analysis to be less than 80 milligrammes/100 millilitres. No one of course knows how many drivers with blood-alcohol levels above 80 escape because their breath does *not* give a positive Alcotest reading.) Because of this margin of error, the Alcotest has been criticised as being insufficiently accurate for its purpose. (See *Day et al.* 1968; and reply by *Wright* 1968—II.) In reply to such criticisms one may however point out: no one has as yet produced a portable, simple and cheap device which is better; even with its admitted margin of error, the Alcotest is likely to be more reliable than a police officer's unaided judgment when the law lays down a blood-alcohol level at which many drivers may not be obviously impaired; the device is intended for on-the-spot operation at the roadside by a police officer by day or night and in all weathers—circumstances in which accurate analysis would be impossible.

The Alcotest is in fact a more sophisticated device than may be apparent. The length from the start of the reagent column to the graduation mark, and the density of packing of the granules, are accurately standardised and controlled in manufacture. The tubes are not sent out by the manufacturer until they have received an extended test for unapparent leaks. Inferior products, some of which are on sale to the public, are liable to have an inconstant column length (making accurate measurement impossible) and to be packed either much too loosely or so tightly that it is practically impossible to blow through them.

Evidence regarding the result of a screening breath test using the Alcotest is of course specifically excluded by the Road Safety Act 1967, s. 1 (except in regard to procedural steps), since the level prescribed by that Act is to be "ascertained from a laboratory test" of blood or urine.

B. BLOOD AND URINE ANALYSIS

The ideal method for the analysis of blood or urine specimens for alcohol would:

(1) Be adequately sensitive, accurate and precise in the hands of any competent analyst. (See the following chapter for the meanings of "accurate" and "precise' in this context.)

(2) Be specific for ethanol.

(3) Be suitable for the routine analysis of large numbers of specimens.

(4) Not require any expensive equipment.

No existing method meets all these criteria, as is shown by the large number of methods that have been proposed and used.

Any method can be classified as either (I) macro (requiring, say, 1-2 millilitres of specimen per analysis); (II) micro (requiring 0·1-0·2 millilitres of specimen, or less, per analysis). All or practically all the existing methods also fall into one of the three classes: (a) chemical; (b) biochemical; (c) physical.

As is now well known, the method currently operated in this country is a gas-chromatographic one—a physical method. Before we describe it, however, the other methods that have been in general use will be very briefly outlined.

Chemical methods

These include both macro- and micro-methods, and are simple, accurate and easy to operate. Macro-methods have been preferred to micro- where the amount of blood or urine available permitted, since they are simpler and less troublesome to use. All are quite satisfactory in respect of criteria (1) and (4) above, and some in respect also of (3). However, as most of them depend on the reduction of a biochromate/sulphuric acid mixture by alcohol vapour, they are essentially methods for the determination of volatile reducing substances, and do not therefore fulfill criterion (2). They can, however, be made adequately specific in forensic practice because : (a) the quantitative determination can be combined with a specific qualitative test for ethanol; (b) very few other volatile reducing substances occur in the blood of living persons; (c) subsidiary tests can be made to confirm the absence of the very few substances which would simulate alcohol in the analysis and which may occur in blood.

The chemical methods which have been most extensively used include :

The original *Widmark* method. This is a micro-method in which the alcohol from a very small sample of blood distils slowly at a fairly low temperature into the bichromate in a small closed vessel.

The *Southgate & Carter* method. This is a macro-method in which the sample is evaporated in an air stream at about 90° C, the air subsequently passing through the hot bichromate reagent, which absorbs the alcohol vapour.

The *Cavett* method is a modification of the *Widmark* one, being also a micro-method but using a different chemical reaction to determine the amount of alcohol vapour absorbed.

The *Kozelka & Hine* method. This is a macro-method in which the alcohol is distilled from the hot sample in a current of steam. The steam is condensed after passing through a subsidiary reagent to trap interfering substances, and the alcohol in the condensate is determined by the reduction of bichromate as a separate step. The removal of interfering substances makes this method more specific than other chemical ones, and it was therefore much used as a checking method when such substances were known or suspected to be present. It is however too time-consuming for the routine analysis of large numbers of specimens.

The *Nickolls* method (often referred to as the "macro-Cavett" method, though "macro-Widmark" would have been a more accurate description). This was similar in principle to the *Widmark* and *Cavett* methods, but, by using a 1-millilitre or 2-millilitre sample, avoided incurring unnecessarily the greater difficulties of micro-methods when ample quantities of urine were normally available for analysis.

Biochemical methods

For all practical purposes, there is only one such method—the *ADH* one. This is a micro-method in which the alcohol is oxidised by the ADH enzyme in the presence of a co-enzyme (see p. 17); the reduced co-enzyme is then determined colorimetrically by a separate operation, from the result of which the alcohol content of the original sample is calculated. In skilled hands the method is extremely accurate. It is also, like all enzymatic reactions, highly specific. The enzyme does react to some extent with two other alcohols chemically closely related to ethanol—namely propanol and butanol; these however do not occur in blood. It does *not* react with methanol, which may occur in the blood of "meths" drinkers.

The method therefore fulfills excellently criteria (1) and (2) above, and has in several parts of the world been used extensively with great success. (For a strong French recommendation, see *Truhaut et al.* 1964.) It can also, according to a recent German claim (*Leithoff et al.* 1966), be "scaled down" for use as an ultra-micro method with as little as 8 microlitres (about one-sixth of a drop) of specimen. However, the second stage of the method requires some moderately expensive equipment, and does have the slight disadvantage that it probably demands for its successful operation a greater degree of skill than chemical methods and that the reagents are expensive and do not keep well. In short, it is extremely satisfactory as an accurate routine method in the hands of skilled analysts, since they "keep their hand in" by doing large numbers of analyses; on the other hand, it is not possible to take advantage of its accuracy and specificity by keeping it as a "reserve" method, since if it is used only occasionally the operators may lose their skill at it and it would also be necessary to make up for each occasion a fresh batch of the expensive reagents necessary.

Physical methods

Again, for all practical purposes there is only one such method—gas chromatography. It fulfils the second and third, and probably the first, criterion mentioned on p. 79 better than any other method, but the equipment for it is admittedly and unavoidably very expensive.

It was adopted as the standard method for analyses made under the Road Safety Act 1967 after a careful investigation of all possible alternatives, and clearly emerged as by far the most suitable, in spite of the expense entailed in equipping for it, its only serious rival being the ADH method. What made it a clear winner was (a) its extremely high sensitivity; (b) its absolute specificity; (c) its speed; (d) its proven accuracy.

Characteristics (a) and (b) were essential since, assuming that the blood specimens to be analysed were skin-puncture capillary ones, the method chosen had to be adequate for very small quantities of blood, with which it would also be impossible to do any other confirmatory tests proving the presence of ethanol.

Characteristic (c) was essential since it was assumed (as has proved to be the case) that many more cases would have to be dealt with than before the Act came into force.

Characteristic (d) was essential since obviously any method used in operating a fixed-level law *had* to be as accurate as was humanly possible.

The gas chromatographic method could fairly within the present context be described as "ultra-micro." The quantity taken for each separate determination is quite extraordinarily minute—of the order of one-fifth of a microlitre of blood or less, containing probably less than half a microgram of alcohol. (One average drop contains about 50 microlitres; an aspirin tablet weighs about 300,000 micrograms.) The actual analysis could indeed be performed on even much smaller quantities, the practical lower limit of sample size being determined not by the capabilities of the equipment but by the difficulty of handling very small samples.

When the methods for operating a fixed-level law were under consideration and investigation in this country, gas-chromatographic ones had not at that time proved to be as accurate and reliable as would be necessary for this purpose. That they could be developed to be so was then only an informed hope. Its realisation

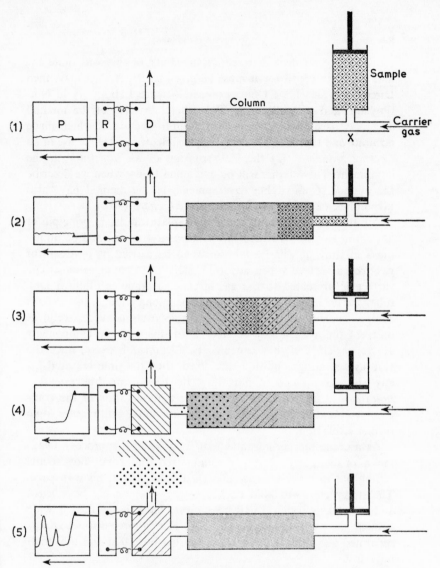

Fig. 11. GAS CHROMATOGRAPHY

The sample to be analysed is injected (1, 2) at X into the stream of carrier gas entering the column. The various constituents of the sample (*e.g.*, ethanol and the internal standard in blood-alcohol analysis by this method) are carried through the column at different rates (3) because they are adsorbed to different extents by the column packing. Hence, if the column is long enough, they emerge separately at different times (4). The detector D, which is sensitive to changes in the composition of the issuing gas, feeds electrical impulses corresponding to these into the recorder R, where they are amplified and converted to pen motions on a moving paper strip P (5).

The magnitude of the signals from the detector is also proportional to the amount of each component issuing from the column, and in blood-alcohol analysis the amplified signals are also fed into an integrator which prints out a number expressing that magnitude.

required a good deal of research; the bulk of this was done by, and the main credit for it must be given to *Dr. A. S. Curry*, then Director of the Home Office Forensic Science Laboratory in Nottingham, and his colleagues. The crucial features of the method developed (see *Curry et al.* 1966), the introduction of which made accurate and reproducible analyses possible, were: (1) the use of an *internal standard*; (2) the incorporation of an *integrator* in the equipment. These terms will be explained below when we describe the method. Comparable developments in the method have also taken place on the Continent. (See *e.g. Machata* 1967.)

An attempt is made in fig. 11 to explain the basic principle of gas chromatography. It depends as an analytical method on allowing a mixture of volatile substances to be carried by a stream of gas past a surface which adsorbs* them to different extents. The surface is presented to the gas stream as granules filling a long tube (the *column*); then, if the column is long enough, the various components of the mixture will emerge from it successively, at different times after they entered it. In this way the components are *separated*, and they can also be *identified* because, once the various operating conditions are fixed, then the time required for any given compound to pass through the column (the *retention time*) is also fixed and knowable. The *determination* of the components—*i.e.* the measurement of their amounts—will require some further explanation.

As a crude but perhaps adequate analogy to this process, imagine a mixed party of big, medium-sized and small boy scouts setting out to cross a sticky ploughed field each at his own pace. The sticky clay will hold back the long-stepping big boys least, and the short-stepping small boys most. Then, if the field is wide enough, the party will arrive at the far side in three distinct groups separated according to their sizes, the big boys first and the small boys last.

The current analytical procedure is then as follows. A small quantity (about 20 microlitres) of the specimen is withdrawn from its container and diluted with an aqueous solution of the internal standard. The dilution ratio, which is usually about 10:1, need not be precisely known but *must* be invariable. This withdrawal and dilution are performed automatically by a single instrument. 1-2

---

* "Adsorption," which should not be confused with absorption, is a physico-chemical process occurring at a surface whereby the adsorbed molecules are bound to the surface by quasi-chemical forces.

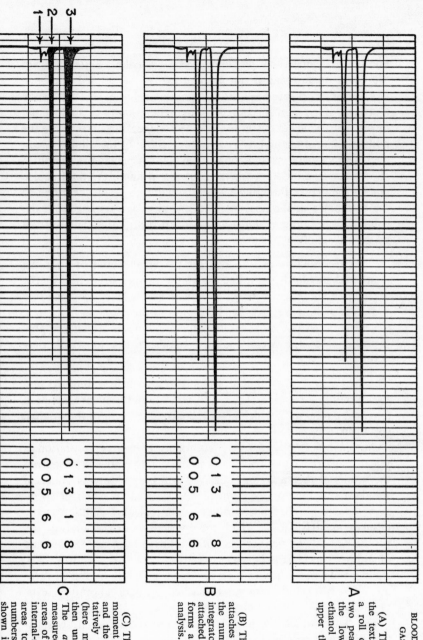

Fig. 12.
BLOOD-ALCOHOL ANALYSIS BY GAS CHROMATOGRAPHY

(A) The equipment described in the text automatically draws on a roll of paper a line showing two peaks. As reproduced here, the lower peak represents the ethanol in the specimen and the upper the internal standard.

(B) The analyst *immediately* attaches a slip of paper bearing the numbers printed out by the integrator. The whole is then attached to the case papers and forms a permanent record of the analysis.

| 0 | 1 | 3 | 1 | 8 |
| 0 | 0 | 5 | 6 | 6 |

(C) The point 1 indicates the moment of injection of the sample, and the ethanol in this is qualitatively identified by the time (here measured vertically) from then until its peak (2) appears. The *amount* of ethanol is measured by the ratio of the areas of the ethanol peak and the internal-standard peak (3). These areas to which the printed out numbers are proportional, are shown in solid black.

microlitres (depending on the expected alcohol content; again the exact quantity need not be known) of the diluted specimen are then injected into the chromatographic column, through which a stream of pure nitrogen is flowing. The column is surrounded by an oven, which keeps it at a selected temperature well above the boiling-point of alcohol, so that vapourisation of the diluted specimen is practically instantaneous. The column packing is of course chosen for its suitability for the purpose in hand, the final choice among the two or three most suitable materials being according to the preference of the analyst. The stream of gas issuing from the column passes into a *flame-ionisation* detector, the signals from which are simultaneously:

(1) recorded as *peaks*—one for the ethanol and one for the internal standard—on a line drawn on a paper strip chart by the *recorder*, the ethanol being identified by the retention time (see above) of its peak (see fig. 12);

(2) printed out by the *integrator* as numbers which are proportional to the areas enclosed by the peaks to which they refer.

The final step is a calculation, using the ratio of these numbers and the currently operative factor for the internal standard solution (see next paragraph), which gives the alcohol content of the original specimen.

An alcohol solution of very accurately known concentration is put through the same whole procedure at frequent intervals; from the results of this, a factor is derived which applies to the internal standard solution for the immediately succeeding batch of specimens analysed. The concentration of this alcohol solution is the ultimate standard upon which the correctness of the analysis depends; that is why neither the initial dilution ratio nor the volume of diluted specimen injected need be accurately known. The standard alcohol solutions used are either prepared by the Government Chemist's Laboratory, or checked by inter-laboratory tests, or both.

The figure which the analyst finally reports (which he is satisfied the true figure is not less than) is the arithmetic mean of the several determinations on the specimen, less three *standard deviations*. The significance of this will be explained in the next chapter.

The three special features of this method which make it a successful one are:

(1) The use of an internal standard. Under completely invariable operating conditions, identical amounts of alcohol passing into the column would always produce identically sized peaks, but it is impossible in practice to keep the operating conditions sufficiently invariable to achieve in this way the accuracy necessary. However, any small variations in the operating conditions will affect the alcohol and the internal standard peaks equally; hence, provided that the dilution ratio is constant (see above), comparison of the two peaks enables the alcohol concentration in the specimen to be accurately determined. The substance chosen as internal standard must be broadly similar to ethanol in its properties, so that it is similarly affected by any small variations in the operating conditions, and must not itself occur in blood taken from living persons. It must also have a retention time sufficiently different from that of ethanol to ensure that the two peaks are clearly separated, but yet, for practical convenience, not so different that one has to wait too long for both substances to emerge from the column. The compound which has been found to comply best with all these conditions is n-propanol, another alcohol closely related to ethanol.

(2) The use of a flame ionisation detector. Other detecting devices are used for other purposes in gas-chromatographic analysis, but no other is so suitable for the present purpose. In a flame ionisation detector, the gas emerging from the column is mixed with hydrogen, which is burned at a jet in a small closed space into which a stream of air is fed. As the ethanol and n-propanol emerge from the column and pass into the hydrogen flame, they alter its electrical conductivity; this is continuously monitored, and the changes are passed on as electrical impulses to the recorder and integrator.

(3) The use of an integrator. This is essentially an electronic device for summing up the total number of impulses received from the detector during the recording of each peak, this number being the determinant of peak size. Therefore the *area* enclosed by each peak on the recorder chart is proportional to the amount of the compound to which it refers. The early experiments on blood-alcohol analysis by gas chromatography used peak *heights*, since these are roughly proportional to peak areas, and more easily measured. However, for various reasons their proportionality is not exact, which makes peak-height measurements inadequate in the present context, especially if results obtained by more than one analyst are to be compared.

Automatic analysis

Manually operated gas chromatography with partial automation of certain stages (*e.g.* dilution) is at present proving extremely satisfactory, but a development which is almost bound to come sooner or later—and sooner rather than later if the work continues to grow at its present rate—is automatic analysis. Automated ADH analysis has apparently proved very satisfactory in Germany.

Nothing is to be gained by entering here and now into a long discussion of possible techniques of automatic analysis, and at this stage a few brief general comments will suffice. With automated techniques, the criteria used in selecting a particular reaction or method as the basis of the analysis are not necessarily the same as with manual techniques, and it may be—without making any definite prognostications—that automated techniques, when they come, will not be just developments of the manual ones successful at present. Automation offers several very attractive advantages over manual operation:

(1) (The most obvious.) Time is saved, so that fewer man-minutes per case are required. This represents a considerable saving when one reflects that the case load in this country is now several tens of thousands per annum.

(2) Automatic methods are quite likely to be more accurate, since machines can be made to work with a precision greater than that of human operators.

(3) The reduced amount of handling of the specimens reduces the risks of getting cases muddled up.

CHAPTER 7

ANALYSIS: ACCURACY

[See note at the beginning of Chapter 5. Also, this chapter deals
with matters which are probably unfamiliar to many readers, but
some understanding of it—a basis for which the writers have
endeavoured to supply—is essential in dealing with a law which
makes a conviction depend upon an analyst's result.]

THERE is of course no such thing as an *absolutely* accurate chemical analysis, or any other sort of measurement. Any measurement
or analysis is subject to *error*, and the important thing is to recognise this fact and to know how large the error is likely to be.

The error of a measurement is the cumulative result of the inherent, inevitable, and individually insignificant small variations
in the operations used in making it. The word "error" has therefore
no pejorative significance in this context. The error must be distinguished from a *mistake*, which is due to carelessness and is avoid-
able. For example, if two cars made the same journey and recorded the distance as 25 and 25½ miles respectively, that variation
is well within the permissible error of mileometers. But if one
driver recorded the distance as 25 miles and the other as 45 miles,
at least one of them has obviously made a mistake.

The absolute error of a measurement will depend upon:

(1) The method of measurement or analysis used.
(2) The skill of the operator.
(3) The expenditure of time and trouble which the circumstances justify.

For the carpenter building a roof, for example, a rule graduated
to (say) eighths of an inch is quite adequate, whereas the engineer
requires a micrometer with which he can measure to the nearest
thousandth of an inch, or even less in modern precision engineer-
ing.

For most purposes, however, it is more useful to know the *proportional* rather than the absolute error—what percentage of the quantity measured does the error represent? (In this respect, the measurements of a ten-foot beam to the nearest quarter-inch, and of the diameter of a half-inch rod to the nearest thousandth of an inch, are of almost exactly the same accuracy.) The proportional error will also depend upon a fourth factor additional to the three mentioned above, namely:

(4) the size of the object being measured or sample being analysed.

For example, if we are weighing something on a balance graduated in half-ounces, the proportional error will obviously be much greater if the object weighs 4 ounces than if it weighs 2 pounds.

In evaluating methods of chemical analysis, two characteristics which it is important to distinguish clearly are *accuracy* and *precision*. The accuracy of a method is determined by how closely its results approach the true ones. The precision of a method is determined by the smallest difference in the quantity being measured which can be detected. It is therefore, with a competent analyst, equivalent to the extent to which successive measurements of the same quantity will yield identical results—that is, *reproducibility*. Precision or reproducibility is therefore a somewhat complex concept, since it depends both on the smallest difference which the method used is capable of detecting, and on the skill of the operator.

The distinction between accuracy and precision is perhaps most simply exemplified by using a watch to tell the time. If this has a correctly synchronised seconds hand, we can tell the time with a *precision* of, say, two or three seconds. The *accuracy* with which we do so, however, depends on whether the watch is right or not; if we have been content to set the watch to the nearest minute, that will be the limit of accuracy. Clearly, we can never make the accuracy greater than the precision and it is pointless to go to the expense and trouble of measurements more precise than the attainable accuracy warrants. If our watch is set only to the nearest minute, we cannot tell the time any more accurately by looking at its seconds hand.

The overall precision of any method of analysis involving several operations also depends upon the precision of the least precise of these. Take as an example the determination of urine alcohol by one of the macro-chemical methods mentioned in the previous chapter. In these, three volumes had to be measured: the specimen of urine, the bichromate reagent, and the volume of another reagent which reacted with the unused bichromate. With suitable apparatus, the first two measurements could easily be made with a precision of perhaps one part in 500, and this was also the attainable accuracy in these measurements, assuming that the apparatus was correctly graduated. The last measurement, on the other hand, was less precise: the volume, which was usually of the order of 5 millilitres, was obtained as the difference between two larger volumes. Neither of these was normally measurable more closely than to the nearest drop, so that the total error in their difference might have been as much as two drops. Since 1 drop = 0·05 millilitre approximately, the precision of this last operation was only about 1 part in 50, (0·1 millilitre in 5 millilitres), as against the 1 in 500 of the first two. The method as a whole, therefore, could not have an accuracy of better than about 2 per cent., and, in any attempt to improve on this, the first two operations could be disregarded and attention concentrated on the last.

There are 4 possible sources of inaccuracy in an analysis:

(1) the precision of the least precise stage in the analysis imposes an ultimate limit upon the accuracy.

(2) There may be systematic errors in the method. It is of course the business of the analyst to detect these, and either to eliminate them or to allow for them. (If we want the correct time, we either set our watch by a time signal or know exactly how many minutes fast or slow it is.)

(3) There may be an undetected fault in the equipment. Again, it is the business of the analyst to make sure that there is not, as far as is humanly possible.

(4) The analyst is human, and his skill, however great, is not infinite. He may make

(a) simple mistakes, such as misreading a number on a scale; or errors of two kinds:

(b) personal systematic errors, such as would be caused by, for example, a persistent tendency to read a scale too high or too low;

(c) errors imposed by the limits of precision with which he personally can make a measurement. If he measures the same thing several times, he will probably not get the same answer every time, in which case his answers cannot all be absolutely correct and none may be. (For example, if he is measuring something of which the true magnitude is 50, he might get 49·8, 50·2, and 50·1.)

Therefore, if we are to make our analyses as accurate as possible, various precautions must be observed. Quite generally, these may include:

A. A detailed study of the method of analysis, from which we may learn about (1) and (2) above.

B. The analysis of reference samples of known composition. This will enable us to detect and eliminate errors due to (2), (3), (4a) and (4b) above, and to evaluate the limit of accuracy imposed by (4c).

C. Repetition of the same analysis by the same analyst. (It is practically unheard of for any analyst ever to give a result unless he has made the analysis at least twice.) This detects errors due to (4a) above, and minimises errors due to (4c).

D. Repetition of the same analysis by two or more independent analysts. This detects errors due to (4a), minimises errors due to (4c) and, except in the very unlikely event of several analysts making the same personal systematic errors, detects errors due to (4b).

All of these precautions should be observed in analyses of blood and urine specimens about which evidence is to be given under section 2 of the Road Traffic Act 1962 or section 3 of the Road Safety Act 1967.

We dealt above with the concept of measurement "to the nearest" so-and-so (one drop in the example cited). This concept carries, however, its own inherent imprecision. Suppose that we have cut for a job of carpentry a number of pieces of wood each 2 feet 6 inches long, and each measured to the nearest $\frac{1}{8}$-inch. We know that, if our rule is accurate and if we have made no mistakes, no piece of wood will be shorter than 2 feet $5\frac{7}{8}$ inches or longer than 2 feet $6\frac{1}{8}$ inches. We do not know, however, whether any are in fact inaccurate by as much as $\frac{1}{8}$-inch, or how many, if any, are in fact exactly 2 feet 6 inches long (or rather, as we have already pointed out that no measurements are ever completely exact, how many are within some smaller selected limit—say $^1/_{64}$-inch—on either side of the nominal length).

The term "experimental error" conveys this meaning of an upper limit to the possible error in a measurement. Figures or measurements are very often given in scientific contexts as "$\pm$" so much. To say that the length of our pieces of wood is $30 \pm \frac{1}{8}$ inches conveys the information about them which has been given at length in the preceding paragraph. By measuring the volume of a liquid to the nearest drop, as in the example quoted above, we could say that it is (say) $15 \cdot 35 \pm 0 \cdot 05$ millilitres. Such information is useful and valuable, and may tell us all that we need to know. However, it is often desirable to know as exactly as possible by how much we may expect the recorded measurement to differ from the true value. This can be achieved, but to do so we must adopt more sophisticated criteria, and must in fact borrow from statistics the concept of *standard deviation*.

Suppose that we make a number of measurements of the same quantity, and assume that there is no *systematic* source of error in our equipment or due to ourselves. Then the inevitable errors in our measurements will be randomly distributed above and below the true value, and the average of our measurements will be as near to the true value as we can get. The standard deviation also tells us, however, the extent to which the individual measurements differ from the mean—presumed true—value. (We are here and in the following paragraphs assuming "mean" and "average" to be synonymous.)

The standard deviation is, in words, the square root of the average of the squares of the deviations of the individual results from their mean. That rather complicated definition (which is not mathematically quite correct, but will suffice for our present purpose) is probably best elucidated by an example. Suppose that 2 analysts, A and B, each make 10 measurements of the same thing. (Again, 10 is rather too small a number for the mathematics to be strictly applicable, but the principle can be illustrated.) Suppose that they get the following two series of results:

Analyst A: 148, 151, 153, 149, 144, 148, 156, 153, 146, 152.

Analyst B: 147, 158, 165, 152, 139, 150, 153, 148, 132, 156.

The average, or arithmetical mean, of both these sets of figures is exactly 150. It is obvious however merely from looking at their results that A is a more reliable analyst than B, in that his individual results are mostly much closer to their mean value than B's are. We would therefore place more reliance on a single measurement made by A than on one made by B.

Let us now calculate the standard deviations according to the verbal formula given above. For A, the deviations of his individual results from their mean are:

—2, +1, +3, —1, —6, —2, +6, +3, —4, +2

and the squares of these numbers are:

4, 1, 9, 1, 36, 4, 36, 9, 16, 4.

The mean of these squares (*i.e.* their sum divided by the number of measurements, which is 10) is 12·0, and the square root of 12·0 is approximately 3·46. The standard deviation of A's results is then 3·46.

A similar calculation gives the standard deviation of B's results as 9·67, which is nearly three times as great as A's. These two figures then give us a measure of the extent to which the two analysts' individual results differ from the presumed true value, and therefore, in one sense, of their reliability as analysts.

It should be noted that the standard deviation can, strictly speaking, be calculated only for results which show a so-called *normal* distribution. This cannot be described precisely in non-mathematical terms, but, roughly, it is the distribution characteristic of measurements showing only random unsystematic errors, with results distributed symmetrically round the mean value and deviations from this value getting progressively fewer as they get larger.

The standard deviation is sometimes referred to as "sigma," from the Greek letter δ by which statisticians designate it. It is also sometimes referred to as the "root mean square," from the way in which it is calculated. In spite of the labour entailed by that calculation, the standard deviation is, because of its important mathematical properties, much more useful as a statistic than the easily calculated *mean deviation*, which is simply the mean of all the deviations (disregarding their signs) from the overall mean. The property of most concern to us here is: if the mean and the sigma of a large number of measurements are calculated, then 68 per cent. (about $\frac{2}{3}$) of all the measurements will lie within one sigma on either side of the mean, 95·5 per cent. (21 out of 22) will lie within 2 sigmas, and 99·73 per cent. (369 out of 370) within 3 sigmas. This means, put in another way: taking a single measurement, the approximate odds are 2 to 1 that it lies within one sigma of the mean (presumed correct) value, 21 to 1 that it lies within 2 sigmas, and 370 to 1 that it lies within 3 sigmas. There is nothing arbitrary or mysterious about all that; it is simply a "built-in" consequence of the arithmetic used in calculating the standard deviation.

When the term "confidence limit" is used in connection with a measurement or series of measurements, it relates to these properties. Since only approximately 5 per cent. of a series of measurements of a quantity will deviate from their mean by more than 2 standard deviations (see above), this range is often quoted at the "95 per cent. confidence limit" for a particular measurement or series of measurements. The importance of this particular figure lies in the fact that, according to a convention generally accepted among statisticians, a statistical result is accepted as *significant* (*i.e.* genuine and meaningful) if there is a 95 per cent. probability that it is not merely the result of random variations in the measurements. (*Cf. e.g.* the results of the Grand Rapids survey described in Chap. 4.)

It must lastly be noted that the standard deviation is a property simply of a particular series of measurements; it is not a property either of the method used to make them or of the operator who made them. However, if an operator practised in a certain method finds that his results for the analysis by that method of a known quantity regularly show a certain standard deviation, then it is a legitimate extension of the meaning to use that standard deviation to predict the degree of accuracy of his results for an unknown quantity.

And this is where we at last return to the analysis of blood or urine specimens for alcohol. By knowing the standard deviation pertaining to the method and/or analyst, we can predict accurately the probability of a particular result lying within any given distance from the true value. For example, since 99·73 per cent. of the results lie within 3 standard deviations of the mean, then if only one analysis was made and three standard deviations subtracted from the result, the odds against the figure so obtained being too high would be approximately 740 to 1. (The odds here are twice those quoted above for three standard deviations, since we start with a 50:50 chance—a probability of $\frac{1}{2}$—of the figure being too low rather than too high.) It would of course be quite improper to rely on only one result, even if this figure were deemed adequate, since it refers only to the inherent irreducible random errors of the method, and takes no account of the possibility of a single *unsystematic* error—a simple mistake, such as mis-reading a figure. This possibility is however eliminated if replicate analyses are made, especially if they are made by independent analysts.

It has been found by extensive trials that, when a competent analyst employing the currently used gas-chromatographic method makes a large number of analyses of the same specimen, the standard deviation of the results is something under 2 per cent. of their mean; with experience, indeed, this figure can be brought down to nearer 1 per cent. In practice therefore:

(1) No one not already qualified by statute (see p. 157) is designated as an "authorised analyst" under the Road Traffic Act 1962 until he has sufficient skill and experience in the method of analysis regularly to get results which show a standard deviation of less than 2 per cent.

(2) A laboratory will not, or should not, accept an analytical result as the basis for a report unless the individual replicate results of which it is the mean show a scatter of not more than three standard deviations. For example (assuming a standard deviation of 2 per cent.), 97, 102, 99, 102 (mean 100), with a total scatter over a range of 5 per cent. would be satisfactory; 96, 105, 104, 95 (mean also 100), with a scatter of 10 per cent., would not. (A particularly careful analyst might well use common sense to make this safeguard even more rigid. If the figures were, say, 99, 100, 99, 105, then, although they all lie within a 6 per cent. scatter, the last figure appears to be "wild" and a further analysis might be made.)

(3) The Home Office, Metropolitan Police and Scottish Home and Health Department authorised analysts in preparing their reports, assume a standard deviation of 2 per cent. They then subtract 6 milligrammes/100 millilitres from all mean figures of 100 or less obtained as under (2), and 6 per cent. of the mean from all figures over 100. Thus, for example, an analytical mean figure of 93 would be reported as "not less than 87", and a figure of 217 as "not less than 204".

It can be calculated that, if these reported figures are derived from the results obtained by two independent analysts each making at least two determinations, and concordant to within the limits given above, then the odds against a final reported figure which just exceeds the legal limit being too high are several millions to 1. For higher figures the odds are of course even greater. This would appear to afford a reasonable guarantee against a miscarriage of justice.

SOME OBJECTIONS ANSWERED

Finally, we give here in summarised form the answers, based on the contents of this and the previous two chapters, to some of the points and objections that may be raised.

(1) The specimens have got muddled up, and the reported figure refers to some other specimen than the defendant's

This is exceedingly improbable if the analyst observes the precautions described in Chapter 5, and in addition (i) checks with his assistant at every stage throughout the analysis the identity of the specimen, and (ii) ensures that the figures have been entered on the appropriate form before the specimen in the next case is opened.

(2) The analyst and/or his assistant have made a mistake, by reading off or writing down a wrong figure, or in their calculations

This would be detected at once by the final results of separate analyses not agreeing, in which case the specimen would be returned for re-analysis. The figures printed out by the integrator (Chap. 6) will also have been attached to the analyst's case papers, so that the arithmetic may be checked independently by someone other than the analyst(s).

(3) The equipment has developed an undetected fault, causing it to produce wrong results.

Faults may occur, but it is hard to see how they could remain undetected. Gas-chromatographic equipment is delicate and sensitive, and requires skilled maintenance, but if it goes wrong the fact is immediately obvious. In any case, (i) the equipment is frequently and regularly checked with alcohol solutions of known concentration (see Chap. 6), (ii) the use of an internal standard ensures that any small variations in the operating characteristics of the equipment do not affect the results, and (iii) if independent analyses are made on separate sets of equipment, any fault in one of these would be at once apparent by the results not agreeing.

(4) The alcohol content of the specimen may have changed because of improper storage and/or too long a delay between taking and analysis

This has been dealt with in Chapter 5. Any change will have

almost certainly produced a loss of alcohol, which cannot therefore prejudice a defendant. However, an additional safeguard is introduced if the results of the analysis of any specimen which has been kept for more than a week are regarded as less reliable.

(5) A blood specimen contained too much plasma, and therefore had a higher alcohol content than whole blood

This point has been dealt with in Chapter 5. The responsibility in this respect must of course rest with the doctor who took the specimen. However, (i) an experienced analyst would notice a different colour at the dilution stage if the blood was seriously deficient in red cells, and (ii) if this has happened, it will have done so because it was difficult to get enough blood from a skin puncture. In that case, there will almost certainly have been a *loss* of alcohol because of too prolonged exposure of the blood to the air at skin temperature (see Chap. 5).

(6) Alcohol has been introduced into the specimen by some accidental contamination

The possibility of contamination by the use of an unsuitable skin sterilisant has been discussed in Chapter 5. Again, responsibility here must of course rest with the doctor. However, as has also been explained in Chapter 5, the fact of such contamination may be detectable on analysis. Contamination with alcohol of a blood specimen from any other source is vanishingly improbable, since it would be almost impossible to add little enough not to produce an analytical figure so high as to be obviously false.

CHAPTER 8

CONVERSION OF BLOOD ALCOHOL TO DRINK TAKEN

THE writers were strongly tempted to make this a one-word chapter: don't. The necessary calculations involve so many approximations and unverifiable assumptions that their results are barely meaningful. However, it is just possible that occasions may arise when some sort of estimate of drink taken is better than none; we therefore give here a brief outline of the subject.

All calculations from blood-alcohol levels to liquor ingested are based on the simple Widmark equation already given in Chapter 2. Tables giving this conversion were formerly published by the British Medical Association (*The Recognition of Intoxication*, 1958). Figures either calculated by the analyst himself or taken from these tables were at one time often given in evidence at the request or even on the insistence of the courts, the members of which usually found a figure of *x* pints of beer or *y* single whiskies more meaningful than a blood-alcohol level.

These quantities of liquor were in fact the quantities which contained the same amounts of alcohol as could be assumed for the various blood-alcohol levels to be present in the whole body of the accused, so that at least these amounts of alcohol must have been drunk. Unfortunately, it proved almost impossible to persuade courts that the quantities were not estimates of the volumes of liquor *actually* consumed. However, as we have already pointed out, the quantities actually drunk must usually be greater than this, and sometimes very much greater. (See *e.g. Rentoul et al.* 1962.)

Such figures were admittedly of some value in prosecutions under the old impairment laws when the calculated quantities were perhaps three or four times what the accused admitted to having drunk. However, although defendants naturally tended to under-estimate their consumptions, such very large discrepancies were unusual.

In short, figures taken from the B.M.A. tables or based on similar calculations were quite unrealistic and generally misleading. Consequently, the B.M.A. have now, in recognition of this fact, omitted such tables from all subsequent publications on drink and driving.

A more recent German attempt to tackle this subject (*Krauland et al.* 1964) has led to the publication of series of tables giving, at various levels of probability, the estimated blood-alcohol levels reached in various sets of circumstances.

If calculations are to be made, it seems better to rely on the simple Widmark equation, remembering that the results cannot be other than approximate and are subject to possibly quite large errors. The equation has already been given, namely

$$a = c \times p \times r.$$

If we take c as the blood-alcohol level found by analysis, p as either the known body weight of the drinker or as the average for his/her sex (men, 11 stones or 70 kilogrammes; women, 9 stones or approximately 55 kilogrammes), and for r, the Widmark factor, assume conservative values of 0·6 for men and 0·5 for women, then a is calculable as a weight of alcohol; it only remains then to further calculate the volume of any specified type of liquor containing this weight of alcohol. Then, obviously, assuming that the calculation of a is valid, not less than this can have been drunk.

We have already pointed out that in the particular case of beer the blood-alcohol level is invariably much lower than that calculated from the amount of alcohol ingested. Therefore, if the liquor taken was beer, it is reasonable to increase by 50 per cent. the quantity as given by the calculation outlined in the previous paragraph—or, which amounts to the same thing, to use for men a Widmark factor of 0·9 instead of 0·6. (Women need not be considered here, since cases of women driving after drinking large quantities of beer are virtually unknown.)

The following table gives for various determined blood-alcohol levels the nominal weights of alcohol which may be assumed to be present in the bodies of (1) men after drinking beer; (2) men after drinking any other liquor; (3) women. The weight given there may then be used in conjunction with the figures given in the last two columns of the table on p. 5 to calculate the minimum volumes drunk of any given type of liquor.

Blood-Alcohol Concentration in mg./100 ml. (c)	Weight of Alcohol in Grams (a)		
	MEN ($p=70$ kg)		WOMEN
	Beer ($r=0.9$)	Other Liquors ($r=0.6$)	($p=55$ kg) ($r=0.5$)
50	31	21	14
60	38	25	16
70	44	29	19
80	50	34	22
90	57	38	25
100	63	42	27
110	69	46	30
120	75	50	33
130	82	55	36
140	88	59	38
150	94	63	41
160	101	67	44
170	107	71	47
180	113	75	49
190	120	80	52
200	126	84	55
210	132	88	58
220	138	92	60
230	145	96	63
240	151	101	66
250	158	105	69
260	164	109	71
270	170	113	74
280	176	118	77
290	183	122	80
300	189	126	82

In making any such calculations, the following points should be borne in mind.

(1) The blood-alcohol level reached after the consumption of any given weight of alcohol will depend on the *weight* of the drinker—the smaller the body throughout which the alcohol is distributed, the less water it contains, and the higher therefore the alcohol concentration in this water. However, it is not worth while attempting to allow for this if the drinker's weight is anywhere near the average, since the variation due to incalculable personal factors is sufficient to make the apparent precision of a

small correction completely spurious. (See *e.g. McCallum & Scroggie* 1963.) It should also be remembered that fat does not absorb alcohol (p. 13), so that the "equivalent" body weight of a drinker who is heavy because he/she is fat will be less than his/her actual weight.

(2) Calculations of this kind are based on the assumption that all the alcohol is ingested within a fairly short time (say, 1 hour or less). If the drinking is spread over a longer period, then more will quite certainly have been drunk than calculation shows.

(3) It is, as previously mentioned, dangerous to make any back-calculation about the blood-alcohol level at any given time prior to sampling. However, if there is a particular reason for making such a calculation, then a fall of 15 milligrammes/100 millilitres per hour should be assumed for the most probable figure, and one of 10 milligrammes/100 millilitres per hour if it is necessary to keep the subsequently calculated quantity of liquor as small as possible.

(4) These calculations may well give an approximately correct figure for fairly strong drink taken within a short time on an empty stomach. In other circumstances however the figure will probably be too low, and *in any circumstances the results, depending as they do on unknown and incalculable personal factors, cannot be accepted as trustworthy. It would be extremely dangerous to attempt to use such calculations to discover how much can be drunk before a fixed blood-alcohol level is exceeded.*

CHAPTER 9

DRUGS AND DRIVING

As we have pointed out elsewhere, the Road Safety Act 1967 is concerned only with the level of alcohol in the blood. Any prosecution for driving whilst under the influence of drugs or a combination of drugs and alcohol must therefore be brought under section 6 of the Road Traffic Act 1960. It will in consequence be necessary to prove actual impairment of driving ability.

Since ethanol is also scientifically speaking a drug, it is perhaps unfortunate that the law has always put "alcohol" and "drugs" in separate categories. However, the practical distinction is clear enough: "alcohol" needs no further definition, whereas a "drug" in the present context is most commonly a pharmaceutical product taken for the relief of some specific ailment or complaint and usually medically prescribed, or, it could be, a pharmacologically active substance taken (often illegally) to relieve stress or "for kicks". The World Health Organisation's Expert Committee on Drug Dependence has defined a drug quite generally as "any substance that, when taken into a living organism, may modify one or more of its functions". (But see also p. 128.)

Information about the effects of drugs on driving ability is by comparison with that available for alcohol extremely scanty. Little or nothing is known about the correlation between driving behaviour and blood concentrations of drugs other than ethanol.

The number of drugs any one of which may have been taken by a driver is very large indeed and constantly increasing, and of these scores and possibly hundreds may affect his driving behaviour. Drugs which may affect driving may be classified in several ways (see *e.g. Rees* 1967; *Goldberg & Havard* 1968; *Bewley* 1969), but the following classification will serve for our present purpose.

Sedatives, including the mild analgesics such as aspirin

By themselves these may be counted harmless, but they are

not infrequently taken in conjunction with more active drugs such as hynotics or stimulants.

Hypnotics: that is, drugs which produce sleep, or lethargy if taken in small doses

The most important members of this group are the barbiturates, which as "sleeping pills" are prescribed for and consumed by a sizeable fraction of the population in vast quantities. Moderately large doses of barbiturates can produce effects resembling alcoholic intoxication—unsteady gait, slurred speech, confusion, etc. The opium drugs (codeine, morphine, heroin), together with cocaine and with their synthetic substitutes such as methadone and pethidine, can also be considered as belonging to this group. These latter are of course notoriously habit-forming and medically are used rather conservatively (indeed heroin is banned altogether in most countries other than Great Britain); they do not however present a serious problem in connection with driving (see below).

Anti-histamines

Anti-histamines are used to relieve allergic urticaria (nettle-rash), insect bites, etc., and by inhalation or in other ways to relieve head cold symptoms. They may produce side effects such as, for example, disturbed vision.

Anti-depressants and tranquillisers

Anti-depressants and tranquillisers are prescribed and consumed today in large quantities to relieve depression or tension. The number offered to the medical profession under various trade names is enormous and constantly increasing. They can produce various side effects undesirable in a driver—chiefly drowsiness. Anti-depressants can also, by lowering the blood pressure, produce dizziness or even fainting.

Stimulants ("pep pills")

Most of these, other than the familiar and relatively harmless caffeine, are derivatives of amphetamine. When properly prescribed they have a limited use in postponing fatigue on exceptional occasions (although their effects at the first time of taking are unpredictable and may be the opposite of those expected). They are notoriously dangerous when taken indiscriminately: large doses can impair motor co-ordination and therefore driving skill, and may also lead to impulsive and possibly criminal behaviour with serious errors of judgment; they also, which is perhaps their chief danger, produce marked depression when their effect wears off, leading to re-medication in increasing doses and eventually psychological dependence.

Psychedelic (or psychomimetic) drugs

The "hard" drugs of the "junkie"—morphine, heroin, cocaine, pethidine, etc.—could in a sense be included here, since they are taken by the addict for the subjective feeling of well-being induced. The drugs with which we are mainly concerned in this group, however, are the so-called "hallucinogens"—chiefly cannabis (also known as hashish, marihuana, "pot" and by many other names) and LSD. The dried cannabis plant, as smoked in "reefers", has no therapeutic use, but tincture of cannabis is sometimes prescribed as a euphoric in the last stages of cancer. Since the euphoria which it is said to produce is coupled with impaired judgment, and since it disturbs perceptions of space and time, driving whilst under its influence could obviously be dangerous. It does not appear to be physically habit-forming. LSD has a limited legitimate use in psychiatry, but the dangers of its illegitimate use are well known: confused judgment, hallucinations, panic, etc. Cases have occurred of persons under its influence killing themselves by falling from high windows out of which they had walked in the conviction that they could fly. There do not seem to have been any cases in this country of persons driving or attempting to drive whilst under its influence, but obviously to do so would be dangerous in the extreme.

Manufacturers are becoming increasingly aware of the effects of the drugs they are marketing, and more and more advertising matter sent out to doctors carries the warning that patients may suffer drowsiness or mild dizziness and should avoid activities requiring optimal alertness. Some adds that the taking of alcohol along with the drug(s) in question may produce similar effects. However, it does seem that some or even many general practitioners do not warn their patients sufficiently forcibly of these dangers. (See e.g. Foster 1967; B.M.A. 1967.)

There are two other points in connection with the effects of drugs which may be mentioned here. One is that the withdrawal of a drug on which a degree of dependence has been acquired (e.g. a barbiturate) may produce marked and unpleasant effects which would be incompatible with safe driving, yet any impairment of driving so produced could not lead to a charge of driving whilst under the influence of drugs, since there might be no trace of the withdrawn drug in the driver's body. The other point concerns the obtaining and holding of a driving licence. The form carries the question whether the applicant "suffers from fits"— presumably to reveal epileptics. An applicant who is a mild epileptic might honestly answer "no" to this question if he is taking regular maintenance doses of phenobarbitone or a similar drug and does not therefore "suffer" from fits. Although the amount of the drug circulating in his body would be minimal, it could probably be detected and even estimated by modern methods of analysis; it is conceivable therefore that such a driver, if he were, say, involved in an accident might find himself in an awkward situation if the drug were detected in a specimen of one of his body fluids.

For reasons which will be discussed below, very few laboratory analyses are in fact done at present in this country in cases of alleged drug-impaired driving. During 1968, for example, the Metropolitan Police Laboratory made such an analysis in only 54 cases (there having been specific requests that they do so in 41 of these), which is well under 1 per cent. of the "drink-and-driving" cases received. Drugs were detected in 20 cases in all. Outside London such analyses are even more uncommon. In the great majority of cases, both in London and the provinces, the drugs detected were barbiturates or tranquillisers. Other drugs such as morphine or one of the amphetamines have occurred merely as isolated instances. As far as the "hard" drugs—morphine, etc.—are concerned, serious as is the social problem which they present, they are of little importance in the present context. The total number of addicts to morphine, heroin, cocaine and pethidine known to the Home Office in 1967 was 1,729, which is a small number compared with the total number of drivers, and in any case (if we can extrapolate from American experience) few addicts are drivers.

A Swedish study of this topic has also been described (*Bonnichsen et al.* 1967). In the 50,000 or more cases of suspected drink-impaired driving occurring in Sweden during the years 1964-66, about 12 per cent. of the drivers stated that they had taken a drug or drugs, with or without alcohol. Chemical analysis was not always requested, and not always made even if requested because the specimens were too small, but it led to the detection of drugs in the specimens submitted in 212 cases in all—rather under $\frac{1}{2}$ per cent. of the total. Barbiturates were detected in 83 of these cases, tranquillisers and related drugs in 53, stimulants in 23 and various other drugs in the remainder. Swedish experience in this matter is therefore very similar to the British.

As we have already said, there is hardly any scientifically ascertained information about the effects of drugs on driving behaviour, and virtually none at all about the effects of various particular blood-drug levels. Alcohol and other drugs may also of course interact, and there has been some investigation of this— not all however concerned with driving, the effect on which must in several cases merely be inferred from the published results. (See *e.g. Aston & Cullumbine* 1959 [animal experiments] and *Eerola & Alha* 1963 [human autopsy material] on fatal combined levels of alcohol with sedatives and hypnotics; *Joyce et al.* 1959 on alcohol/barbiturate interaction and *Miller et al.* 1963 on alcohol/tranquilliser interaction, in both cases at low dosages.) *Carpenter & Varley* (1962) examined the earlier literature on the combined effects of alcohol and tranquillisers on driving without finding any clear conclusions or indeed much positive helpful information. *Im Obersteg & Bäumler* (1967) analysed blood and urine samples from 328 Swiss victims of traffic and other accidents, and found alcohol in 19 per cent. of the cases and other drugs in 4 per cent.; they confirmed what was already known about the connection between alcohol and accidents, but could find no similar connection in the case of drugs.

However, the danger of combining barbiturates in particular with alcohol is now empirically well known. (See *e.g. Buttle, Fearn & Hodges* 1963; *B.M.A.* 1953.) It is uncertain on the available evidence whether these substances merely exhibit synergism, so that their combined effect is merely the sum of their individual effects (*B.M.A., loc. cit.; Eerola & Alha, loc. cit.*), or whether they potentiate each other, so that their combined effect is greater than the sum of their individual effects (*Joyce et al., loc. cit.*). The point is however rather an academic one.

There has been a little research specifically on the actual or inferential effect on driving of combining of alcohol and various other drugs, chiefly tranquillisers. *Loomis* (1962), using the equipment which he and West had used for alcohol experiments (Chap. 4), tested the effects of secobarbitone, meprobamate and chlorpromazine (the last two being both tranquillisers) on subjects whose blood-alcohol levels were maintained as nearly as possible at 100 milligrammes/100 millilitres. He found that measurable impairment could be produced by these drugs, either alone or in conjunction with alcohol, but only when they were given in doses larger than the normal therapeutic ones. *Goldberg* (1965), using an elaborate series of clinical and psychological tests on subjects receiving a combination of alcohol and amphetamine or one of several tranquillisers, showed mainly that the problem was an extremely complex one. He found that the nature and extent of the interaction depended both on the identity of the other drug and on the phase of the blood-alcohol curve at the time of the test. Drugs producing by themselves clinically similar effects might interact in quite different ways with alcohol. Alcohol-amphetamine interactions in non-driving situations have also been studied by the Indiana University researchers in this field (*Kaplan et al.* 1965; *Brown et al.* 1965). Taken alone, the amphetamines improved and alcohol impaired performance, as was to be expected. When they were taken together, performance was, after an initial short period of relative improvement, no better than with alcohol alone—that is, alcohol appeared to suppress the effect of the other drug. Finally, a further exhaustive study by an impressive team of investigators (*Kielholz, Goldberg, Im Obersteg et al.* 1967) of the interaction of alcohol and two popular tranquillisers, using the same car-handling tests as Bjerver & Goldberg had used in 1951 for alcohol alone (see Chap. 4), merely confirmed their previous results for alcohol and showed no effect by the other drugs. They themselves concluded that the effects of higher doses should be tested.

As the law stands at present, a request to the laboratory to analyse a specimen of blood or urine for drugs would probably be made only in the following circumstances: (1) there was evidence of impaired driving, but the breath test for alcohol proved entirely negative; (2) the breath test showed a blood-alcohol level under 80, but there was clinical evidence of gross impairment such as would normally be associated with a much higher blood-alcohol level; (3) the driver admitted having taken some drug, or sought to explain his behaviour by alleging an unusually large effect of a small amount of drink.

As we have already stated, any charge brought in these circumstances would have to be one of impairment under the Road Traffic Act 1960, and therefore a medical examination should and almost certainly would be made. If the breath test had been negative, then of course any clinically observable signs of intoxication would suggest the effect of a drug by exclusion. However, if any alcohol at all was present, it is probably safe to say that no doctor would be prepared to offer an opinion as to how far the observable effects were due to the alcohol and how far to a drug.

Assuming that a drug is or drugs are suspected, there are several reasons why it may be difficult to get effective scientific evidence in support of a charge.

(1) Since nothing is known about the correlation of blood-drug levels and impairment (see above), an analysis (assuming that one is possible—see below) can merely confirm the presence of a drug (or of its metabolite) the taking of which would be consistent with the clinically observed effects.

(2) Analysis for drugs other than ethanol requires very much larger specimens than those normally taken under the Road Safety Act 1967. This is because (a) most drugs, being pharmacologically much more potent than ethanol and therefore taken in much smaller quantities, are present in body fluids in much smaller concentrations; (b) the analysis, unlike that for alcohol, may not be a simple determination of an expected specific substance, but may involve also the identification of the drug, if any, present. While it may be possible in exceptionally favourably circumstances to determine a specific drug present in relatively large amount in 1-2 millilitre quantities of a body fluid, in general an analysis for "a drug" will require at least 20 millilitres of specimen and preferably 50 or more.

Urine is particularly suitable as a fluid for this purpose— ample is normally available and it is in any case the best fluid for general "screening" tests. Drug analysis required therefore only skill and time when urine was the fluid normally submitted. Indeed, an analysis for drugs was often made as a matter of course whenever a very low alcohol figure was found although there was a case history of obvious impairment. This source of information is not available when only small blood samples are taken.

Unfortunately it is not possible to compel a driver to supply specimens of *both* blood and urine. Although, as we have already indicated, prosecutions for driving under the influence of drugs must be brought under the impairment offence, the powers conferred by section 3 of the Road Safety Act 1967 to require blood *or* urine specimens for laboratory tests are applied by that section also to impairment cases, and so are available alongside section 2 of the Road Traffic Act 1962. None of these provisions however permits greater demands to be made than in any other case: that is to say, blood may be demanded, or urine, but not both. If the accused consents there can be no serious objection to specimens of both blood and urine being supplied, but difficulties might possibly be encountered if it later became necessary in such a case to distinguish which specimen had been taken under the powers in the Act and which gratuitously supplied. This difficulty would partly at least be overcome if in any amending legislation power was given, where impairment by drugs was suspected, to require both blood and urine specimens from the accused driver.

The analysis of blood or urine specimens for drugs forms part of the methodology of toxicological analysis, and is too large and complex a subject to be dealt with here. In general, the analysis may involve preliminary screening tests for the presence of drugs and provisional clues as to their identity, followed by identification and determination using all the available modern analytical techniques.

Carbon monoxide

This notoriously poisonous gas is not of course a drug, but it is convenient to mention it here. It may form up to about 6 per cent. of car exhaust gases; it may therefore constitute a hazard in a closed car, coming either from a leaky exhaust system of the car itself, or (more probably) by being sucked in by a heater fan from the exhaust of the car in front in a stationary line of traffic, and this reason is sometimes advanced as a cause of apparent intoxication in a driver.

A healthy person can stand 5-10 per cent. saturation of his blood with carbon monoxide without noticeable effects, whilst the fatal dose varies from about 30 per cent. saturation for the aged and sufferers from heart disease to about 75 per cent. for a healthy young adult. One may therefore perhaps guess (no figures are available) that the saturation level in an otherwise healthy person whose driving is impaired for this reason might be of the order of 20 per cent. Some rather tenuous support for this estimate is given by the figures for American accident victims published by *Sunshine et al.* in 1968.

Clinically, carbon monoxide poisoning can closely resemble alcoholic intoxication, except that it does not produce nystagmus. Nothing is known of the combined effect of carbon monoxide and alcohol, but *Sunshine et al.* (*loc. cit.*) suggest that an additive effect may be presumed. This conclusion is tentatively supported by *Fazekas & Rengei* (1969) from their investigation of human fatal cases and from their animal experiments. The results of investigations into the effects of carbon monoxide poisoning on the course of the blood-alcohol curve are inconclusive, but the most trustworthy seem to show that there is no effect (*Elber & Schleyer*, p. 103).

Carbon monoxide can easily be determined in quite small blood specimens provided that they are taken within a short time of the exposure to the gas and that they are tightly sealed. It is doubtful however whether the specimens taken under the Road Safety Act 1967 would be large enough, and in any case no laboratory would make this examination unless specifically requested, as the method of analysis is totally different from those used for alcohol or drugs.

The preceding discussion is in fact somewhat academic, chiefly because carbon monoxide disappears fairly rapidly from the blood when exposure to it has ended and pure air is being breathed; recovery therefore is rapid and a blood sample unless taken almost at once would not show its presence in significant amount. Even if we assume therefore that carbon monoxide poisoning may be retrospectively suspected if

(1) the breath test for alcohol is negative, *and*
(2a) the driver claims that he was affected by exhaust fumes,
or (2b) the medical examination suggests this possibility, alcohol being absent and the driver showing a rapid recovery,

it is unlikely that this suspicion would have become firm enough in time for the taking of an adequate blood specimen to be useful.

If, however, in these circumstances the driving was sufficiently impaired for the police to consider charging the driver with some traffic offence not concerned with drink or drugs, and if he alleged that a faulty exhaust in his own car was responsible for his impairment, then the air inside the car should be tested for carbon monoxide with the engine running and the windows shut. Any forensic science laboratory would probably be willing to do this, but it would of course mean depriving the driver of his car for at least a day.

CHAPTER 10

EFFECTS OF ALCOHOL ON THE DRIVER: ATTEMPTS AT STATUTORY DEFINITION

"DRUNK IN CHARGE"

THE law has long taken cognisance of excessive drinking. The offence of being "drunk and incapable" was recognised in statute law and in many local private Acts in the eighteenth and nineteenth centuries. Though drunkenness itself was not directly penalised, the anti-social results of persistent and public drunkenness and of drunkenness of those in charge of dangerous machinery, animals and the like were proscribed. Statutory recognition was given by the Licensing Act 1872, s. 12, (and the Licensing (Scotland) Act 1903, s. 70) to the offence of being drunk in charge of any carriage, horse, cattle or steam engine. The 1872 Act provisions as to drunk and disorderly behaviour will be replaced in England by those of the Criminal Justice Act 1967, s. 91, which gives power of arrest without warrant, though this section is not yet in force. Legislation subsequent to 1872 imposed penalties for drunkenness in those having positions of special responsibility such as engine drivers, ships' masters, pilots, taxi-drivers and service personnel.

The Criminal Justice Act 1925, s. 40, penalised a person drunk while in charge on any highway or other public place of any mechanically propelled vehicle, and this enactment may be regarded as the foundation of the modern English attempts to control the drinking driver. Because of the terms used it is likely that only a fairly gross degree of drinking could be brought within the scope of the offence, and when in *R. v. Presdee* (1927) 20 Cr. App. R.95 it was confirmed that "drunk" in the 1925 Act meant drunk as it is commonly understood (see also *R. v. Burdon* (1927) 20 Cr. App. R.80), it became clear that the time was ripe for a more precise definition of the driving offence. For similar reasons it is clear that the expression "drunk" ought no longer to be used in describing the modern offence: *R. v. Carr* (1934) 24 Cr. App. R. 199. The opportunity for re-definition might, following Continental law, have led to an emphasis on the element of public danger resulting in injury or death, but instead the wider concept of impairment of general driving control was chosen: (*Lasok*).

"UNDER THE INFLUENCE OF DRINK OR DRUGS"

In the event, the increasing flow of motor traffic following the First World War and the urgent need for closer control produced the Road Traffic Act 1930 which, recognising that it was not necessary to be drunk to be a danger to road-users, re-defined the offence in the following terms in section 15(1):

> "Any person who, when driving or attempting to drive or when in charge of a motor vehicle on a road or other public place is under the influence of drink or a drug to such an extent as to be incapable of having proper control of the vehicle . . . [shall be guilty of an offence]"

This statute thus established a single offence applicable throughout Scotland, England and Wales, triable both summarily and on indictment. (For the law affecting Northern Ireland see *Hagan & Osborough*.) In such circumstances the desirability of uniform construction of the law is obvious: *cf. Cording* v. *Halse* [1955] 1 Q.B. 63. Despite this the differences in legal systems north and south of the Border produced practical results which brought about a more critical situation in England and Wales than that which obtained in Scotland. According to English practice, since the maximum possible sentence exceeded three months imprisonment the accused over fourteen years of age if proceeded against summarily could claim trial by jury (see now the Magistrates' Courts Act 1952, s. 25), an option which was sometimes exercised despite the possibility of heavier sentence on conviction. The reason seemed to be that juries, mainly composed of motorists, tended to sympathise with the driver and, as events proved, were rather unwilling to convict even in serious cases. Moreover the use of the word "incapable" provided an unfortunate reminder of the old offence of "drunk and incapable" and some juries looked for a standard of gross drunkenness which the law certainly did not intend. The proportion of convictions by judges turned out to be significantly higher than that of juries in similar cases. In Scotland where section

15 cases were brought almost exclusively in the summary courts there was no option for jury trial and convictions were more readily obtained (see "Chemical Tests, etc." [*Murphy* 1964]). There was moreover growing concern throughout the country that the figures returned by the police for accidents caused by the effects of drink did not reflect the true proportions of the problem, partly because of the diffidence of English juries, and partly because the police could attribute to drink only those cases where there was conclusive evidence of drink and nothing else. In 1951, for example, the figure for accidents caused through drink was a mere 1,300. Figures of this kind seriously understated the problem and ceased to be relied upon. (*Cf.* also pp. 44-45 and 52.)

The definition of the offence of driving, attempting to drive or being in charge while under the influence of drink or drugs which we have quoted nevertheless served for over twenty-five years. In time, however, the enormously increased number of vehicles using the congested roads of these islands together with the difficulties of proving by observer evidence and the results of clinical examination that a particular driver was "under the influence" combined to lead the British Medical Association in 1951 to revive an earlier Committee to review their publications on testing for drunkenness and on the relation of alcohol to road accidents.

In 1954 this Committee produced a report "The Recognition of Intoxication" in which they recorded their belief that many accidents were caused by persons whose degree of intoxication was insufficient to attract the attention of the police, and yet whose skills were sufficiently impaired to constitute a danger on the road. The report also included a model outline clinical examination the main purpose of which was to exclude any possibility of the accused's condition being due to illness. The clinical examination included tests for lack of co-ordination and alertness as well as for the more obvious manifestations of excessive drinking. The 1954 report went on to consider the better techniques then becoming available for analysis of the alcohol concentration of body fluids, and the experience of this work gained in particular by the Scandinavians. Conversion tables were provided which were thought to enable some estimate to be made of the minimum intake of alcohol required to yield particular urine or blood-alcohol figures.

In 1956 the Road Traffic Act of that year by section 9 separated the offence of driving while under the influence of drink or drugs from that of being in charge of (but not driving) a vehicle while under the influence. It gave the expression "unfit to drive" as meaning "under the influence of drink or a drug to such an extent as to be incapable of having proper control of a motor vehicle" and brought pedal cyclists not under the new law but under the offence as it had been defined in the 1930 Act (see now the Road Traffic Act 1960, s. 11). A revised edition of the B.M.A. report on "Recognition of Intoxication" issued in 1958 repeated its suggested scheme of medical examination, emphasising that it offered no more than a guide to clinical examination, and devoted some attention to the re-defined offence of driving "under the influence".

In 1960 the B.M.A. Committee produced a further report "Relation of Alcohol to Road Accidents" in which the accumulating evidence as to the effect of small quantities of alcohol on driving performance and related skills and also the statistical evidence linking accidents to alcohol intake were examined. This report contained an interesting table giving in brief the situation in other countries and showing that Finland, West Germany, Iceland, Norway, Sweden, Switzerland and some states of the United States of America had adopted mandatory blood testing to provide evidence of impairment based upon blood alcohol concentration. Of these countries some prescribed no limit while others adopted fixed levels beyond which driving impairment was presumed. The report advocated reform of the United Kingdom law by fixing an arbitrary level above which an offence would be committed. A more relaxed description of the drink-driving laws of these and other foreign countries was later provided by *K. M. Bowden.* See also the paper by *Breitenecker.*

In recommending a prescribed alcohol level offence the Committee were endeavouring to reach out towards an objective standard which had previously been lacking in the law, for as well as being tautologous and confusing in its use of the expression "drink or a drug," as though alcohol were not a drug, the 1930 definition, even when amended in 1956, still associated in the lay mind the idea of being under the influence with the idea of gross drunkenness which the law had used in its first attempt to designate the offence.

"Unfit Through Drink or Drugs"

There followed a further amendment whereby the offences were by the Road Traffic Act 1960, s. 6, re-stated (with a statutory defence to the "in-charge" offence) as follows:

(1) A person who when driving or attempting to drive a motor vehicle on a road or other public place, is unfit to drive through drink or drugs shall be liable . . . [to certain penalties].

(2) A person who when in charge of a motor vehicle which is on a road or other public place (but not driving the vehicle) is unfit to drive through drink or drugs shall be liable . . . [to certain penalties].

A person shall be deemed for the purposes of this sub-section not to have been in charge of a motor vehicle if he proves—

(i) that at the material time the circumstances were such that there was no likelihood of his driving the vehicle so long as he remained unfit to drive through drink or drugs; and

(ii) that between his becoming unfit to drive as aforesaid and the material time he had not driven the vehicle on a road or other public place.

"IMPAIRMENT"

The final amendment of the offence of unfitness which had been established by section 6 of the 1930 Act was effected by the Road Traffic Act 1962 whose most important provision in this connection states (section 1):

"For the purposes of section 6 of the principal Act (which imposes penalties for driving, attempting to drive, or being in charge of a motor vehicle while unfit through drink or drugs) a person shall be taken to be unfit to drive if his ability to drive properly is for the time being impaired."

Attention was thus switched from unfitness to drive the vehicle to impairment of driving ability, and the offence now apparently penalises any diminution whatever in proper driving ability. Together with the provisions of section 2 of the Road Traffic Act 1962, which require the court to have regard to the proportion of alcohol or drug in a driver's body as evidenced by blood and urine tests, and permit refusal of such tests to be treated as supporting the prosecution case, (see the discussion at p. 156) these amendments now bring the section 6 offence into its modern and still subsisting form. No guidance whatever was given as to the degree of impairment to be imputed to different alcohol levels and it is possible to criticise the chemical testing law as leaving too many variables to the individual expert (*Murphy*). At all events this left only the B.M.A.'s recommendation for fixed-level legislation to set up an offence which could be easily and undeniably proved still to receive attention.

THE PRESCRIBED ALCOHOL LEVEL

Despite its introduction of powers to require courts to have regard to analytical evidence of blood and urine-alcohol levels, the 1962 Act failed to bring about widespread reliance upon these methods of proof, and observation of the driver's conduct coupled with clinical examination remained the standard method of proving the offence of unfitness and impairment of ability to drive. Analytical evidence was restricted mainly to urine specimens, and where blood was used the specimens had to be large enough to permit of macro-analysis. The fact that courts were inexperienced in interpreting (and indeed without expert evidence could not interpret) evidence that blood-alcohol had reached a particular figure and the difficulties of translating urine-alcohol to blood-alcohol concentrations combined to restrict the use made of scientific evidence. Efforts were made in some cases to calculate back from the levels demonstrated to show that a given quantity of alcohol had been taken, but the tables which had been supplied since 1954 in the B.M.A. reports gave, particularly in conditions of social drinking, a most unrealistic picture (*The Drinking Driver* 1965). Accordingly the giving in evidence of quantities of liquor so calculated came to be recognised as misleading and unreliable. (See Chap. 8.)

The answer to these difficulties was eventually provided on the lines recommended by the B.M.A. by the introduction of a fixed level offence. The White Paper on Road Safety Legislation 1965-66 clearly set out the Government's intentions, and after a false start when the first Road Safety Bill of January 1966 lapsed on the dissolution of the Government, a second Bill was introduced later in the year and passed into law with only a modification of the original random testing proposed by the White Paper.

The new offence, which will be more fully described later, is one of driving or attempting to drive a motor vehicle on a road or other public place, alcohol having been consumed in such a quantity that the proportion thereof in the blood as ascertained from a laboratory test exceeds the prescribed limit at the time of sampling, which at present is set at 80 milligrammes of alcohol per 100 millilitres of blood: Road Safety Act 1967, s. 7. This offence does not supersede the offence of driving while ability is impaired through drink or drugs but is supplementary to it. There is no provision to prevent conviction for both offences. The present situation therefore is that the law distinguishes the offence of driving or attempting to drive while the ability to drive is for the time being impaired by drink or drugs (which we have called the impairment offence), as well as the offence of being in charge of a vehicle in such a state, from the complementary offences of driving or attempting to drive while the driver's blood alcohol concentration exceeds the prescribed limit (which we have called the prescribed level offence) or being in charge of a vehicle in that condition.

The new law contained in the Road Safety Act 1967 is applied by section 6 to vehicles and persons in service of the Crown, and shall apply abroad as well as within Great Britain to persons subject to service discipline.

These offences will be more fully considered in the following chapter.

CHAPTER 11

THE PRESENT OFFENCES

ESSENTIAL ELEMENTS

"Motor Vehicle": "Driving": "Road"

The Road Traffic Acts and the related legislation deal with driving or being in charge of motor vehicles upon the roads or other public places, and some account must be given of how these terms have come to be defined.

The offences of driving a motor vehicle while unfit through drink or drugs on a road or other public place (Road Traffic Act 1960, s. 6—the impairment offence) and driving a motor vehicle on a road or other public place having consumed alcohol in such quantity that the blood alcohol concentration exceeds the prescribed limit (Road Safety Act 1967, s. 1—the prescribed level offence) imply certain essential elements. The most important of these are the terms "motor vehicle," "driving" and "road or other public place."

In the ordinary way the least uncertainty is likely to apply to the term "motor vehicle" defined by the Road Traffic Act 1960, s. 253(1) as "a mechanically propelled vehicle intended or adapted for use on roads." The vast majority of drink and driving offences involve either private cars or commercial vehicles. It should be noted however that mechanical dumpers have been held excluded from the definition since they are not generally adapted for use on the public roads (*cf. MacDonald* v. *Carmichael*, 1941, J.C. 27; *Daley* v. *Hargreaves* [1961] 1 All E.R. 552; *MacLean* v. *McCabe*, 1964 S.L.T. (Sh. Ct.) 39 as have Go-karts (*Burns* v. *Currell* [1963] 2 Q.B. 433; *Chalgray Ltd & Anor.* v. *Aspley* [1965] Crim. L.R. 440) although where these unsuitable contraptions do venture on to the highway especially in unsteady hands they are probably a greater danger than regular vehicles. But an earth scraper seems to fall within the definition of a motor vehicle (*Childs* v. *Coghlan* (1968) 112 S.J. 175) as does a road roller (*Waters* v. *Eddison Steam Rolling Co.* [1914] 3 K.B. 818). One is tempted to wonder why case law throws no light on the powered lawn mower until one realises that this is specifically excluded from the definition by the Road Traffic Act 1960, s. 254. A defective vehicle may be repaired so that it remains a "motor vehicle"—*Elliott* v. *Grey* [1960] 1 Q.B. 367—even when the engine is removed—*Newberry* v. *Simmonds* [1961] 2 Q.B. 345; but a stage may be reached at which a canni-balised hulk is no longer repairable and ceases to fall within the definition; *Smart* v. *Allan* [1963] 1 Q.B. 291; *MacLean* v. *Hall*, 1962 S.L.T. (Sh. Ct.) 30.

"Driving" is also a concept which is unlikely to give much trouble It implies having some control either of steering or of propulsion: *R.* v. *Roberts* (No. 2) [1965] 1 Q.B. 85. Where these acts are shared as in driving instruction each participant is regarded as a driver (*cf.* s. 257 of the 1960 Act): *Langman* v. *Valentine* [1952] 2 All E.R. 803; *R.* v. *Wilkins* (1951) 115 J.P. 443; *Evans* v. *Walkden* [1956] 3 All E.R. 64, as was a person who released the handbrake of a lorry and coasted it down a hill: *Saycell* v. *Bool* [1948] 2 All E.R. 83, and even a passenger who set a vehicle in motion by switching on the ignition and starting the engine while the gears were en-gaged: *R.* v. *Levy* [1956] Crim. L.R. 340. In general the person who steers a towed vehicle is not driving: *Wallace* v. *Major* [1946] K.B. 473. Where a vehicle pushed from behind was steered con-flicting decisions have been rendered as to whether the steersman was driving: *R.* v. *Spindley* [1961] Crim. L.R. 486: *R.* v. *Arnold* [1964] Crim. L.R. 664. In the case of *Ames* v. *MacLeod* [1969] Jo. Crim. Law 55 (on appeal to High Court) the person pushing and steering a vehicle through the open window backwards down a slope was held to be driving. The act of driving requires volition and the English courts have had to consider whether the onset of disease might produce a state of automatism proof of which by the party alleging it would relieve of criminal liability: *Hill* v. *Baxter* [1958] 1Q.B. 277 and in that case the judges figured such a situation as where the hapless driver was attacked by a swarm of bees. It would seem that such a state could hardly be sustained over any substantial distance without amounting to driving: *Wat-more* v. *Jenkins* [1962] 2 Q.B. 572. The Scottish courts have been at pains to make clear that nothing short of insanity is likely to negative the responsibility of the driver *H. M. Advocate* v. *Cunning-*

ham, 1963 S.L.T. 345. The case of a driver suffering a slight stroke at the wheel does not yet seem to have arisen. But see *Glanville Williams*. In *R.* v. *Kitson* (1955) 39 Cr. App. R. 66 (C.C.A.) however the accused who awoke from a drunken sleep in the passenger seat of a moving driverless vehicle and resourcefully guided it by steering erratically into the verge was held to have driven the vehicle.

A specially extended meaning for the term "driving" has had to be adopted in construing the Road Safety Act 1967 (see p. 134, *infra*).

It was clearly established in the case of *Harrison* v. *Hill*, 1932 J.C. 13 that the definition of "road" adopted by the Road Traffic Act 1930 and which is repeated in the 1960 Act included places to which the public had access by permission or tolerance but not those in which they had to trespass to gain entry: *cf. R.* v. *Waters* (1963) 107 S.J. 275. The addition of the words "or other public place" connotes a significant extension. A car park may not be a road as understood by the Acts (*cf. Griffin* v. *Squires* [1958] 3 All E.R. 468 (D.C.), where there was a free public car park to which the public had access) but may yet be a "public place" in which it is an offence to drive while proper driving ability is impaired through drink or drugs or while the blood-alcohol concentration exceeds the permitted level. A forecourt serving for delivering goods though not for through passage is not a road: *Henderson* v. *Bernard*, 1955 S.L.T. (Sh. Ct.) 27: *cf. Thomas* v. *Dando* [1951] 2 K.B. 620, *MacNeill* v. *Dunbar*, 1965 S.L.T. (Notes) 79, and *Purves* v. *Muir*, 1948 J.C. 122. A titled English landowner who drove while in such a state on the estate policies over which the public had access to view his stately home would almost certainly be committing an offence, as would even a recluse Scotsman driving up his private avenue: *Davidson* v. *Adair*, 1934 J.C. 37 whether or not the public were admitted. But the latter factor is vital in England. So a field used for a point-to-point meeting was a public place: *R.* v. *Collinson* (1931) 23 Cr. App. R. 49; and one at an agricultural show: *Paterson* v. *Ogilvy*, 1957 J.C. 42, *MacDonald* v. *McEwan*, 1953 S.L.T. (Sh. Ct.) 26 and the car park behind an inn: *Elkins* v. *Cartlidge* [1947] 1 All E.R. 829; but the matter is one requiring evidence of the public's access: *Williams* v. *Boyle* [1963] Crim. L.R. 204, and the intention is to protect those who resort there, however few: *R.* v. *Warren* (1932) 96 J.P.J. 301; *R.* v. *Waters* (1963) 107 S.J. 275. See also *Hogg* v. *Nicholson*, 1968 S.L.T. 265.

See further the section "What is a Road" at [1959] Crim. L.R. 326.

Attempts

Attempting to drive while the ability properly to do so is impaired by drink or drugs, and attempting to drive while the blood alcohol level exceeds the prescribed limit are both specific offences. In *R.* v. *Cook* [1964] Crim. L.R. 56 a man caught in the driving seat with the dashboard lit and fiddling with the ignition was convicted of attempting to drive whilst impaired.

In charge

Although the 1930 Road Traffic Act treated the offence of driving while under the influence of drink or a drug on the same basis as that of being in charge of a vehicle while under the influence of drink, its failure to distinguish the quality of culpability gave rise to criticism. Accordingly the Road Traffic Act 1956, s. 9, separated the offence of being in charge from the principal offence and treated it more leniently. This approach was continued by the 1960 Road Traffic Act which, when it came to re-define the driving offence, maintained the separation of the offence of being in charge. In addition that statute provided a specific defence for in-charge cases where (a) there was no likelihood of the vehicle being driven so long as unfitness persisted, and (b) no driving had in fact taken place since impairment. The second of these qualifications was repealed by the Road Safety Act 1967, s. 1(5), presumably to encourage drivers on feeling the effects of drink to cease driving and more readily bring themselves within the scope of the in charge offence.

Alongside the impairment offence for driving there accordingly stands the different and lesser (*cf. Jones* v. *English* [1951] 2 All E.R. 853) offence of being in charge whilst impaired. To this charge there is a statutory defence similar to that just mentioned, that at the material time circumstances were such that there was no likelihood of the accused driving so long as he remained unfit to drive through drink or drugs. The onus of establishing such a defence rests upon the accused and would normally require evidence from him sufficient to satisfy the court on a balance of probabilities. The case of *Thaw* v. *Segar*, 1962 S.L.T. (Sh. Ct.) 63 in which it was said that the standard demanded was proof beyond reasonable doubt, has recently been disapproved in *Neish* v. *Stevenson* [1969] S.L.T. 229 when the statutory defence to a charge under section 1(2) of the Road Safety Act 1967 was under consideration. In general something more than intention not to drive must be proved *Morton* v. *Confer* [1963] 2 All E.R. 765 and delivery of the ignition key to another party is often an element in such cases— *e.g. Farrell* v. *Campbell*, 1959 S.L.T. (Sh. Ct.) 43—though perhaps not an invariable one: *R.* v. *Harnett* [1955] Crim. L.R. 793. Merely to immobilise the engine may not be sufficient for there can conceivably be driving, *Saycell* v. *Bool* [1948] 2 All E.R. 83. and therefore possibly being in charge, without the engine having been started. The comparable and lesser offence of being in charge while exceeding the prescribed blood-alcohol limit—Road Safety Act 1967, s. 1(2), was also created alongside the offence of driving while exceeding that and a rather similar statutory defence section 1(3):

> "A person shall not be convicted under this section of being in charge of a motor vehicle if he proves that at the material time the circumstances were such that there was no likelihood of his driving it so long as there was any probability of his having alcohol in his blood in a proportion exceeding the prescribed limit."

The court may in considering this defence (though not in the case of the "in charge" variant of the impairment offence), disregard the fact that the accused may have been injured or his vehicle damaged, so that it will not prejudice an accused that his being in charge has resulted in a spectacular accident or injury. The wording of sub-sections 1(3) and 1(4) suggests that one or the other, but not both, may be disregarded. It is to be noted that the in-charge offence is not an alternative to which the prosecution may automatically resort in the event of their failing to establish that an accused was driving whilst impaired or over the prescribed limit; they are different substantive offences. Alternative charges may of course be preferred.

There is some varied case law on what constitutes being in charge, much of it relating to the original variant of the principal offence. This, although it may be of assistance in considering the modern offences of being in charge, must be applied with care. In *Crichton* v. *Burrell*, 1951 J.C. 107 for instance Lord Keith said that "the words 'in charge' mean being responsible for the control or driving of the car . . . the person who is for the time being in control of the vehicle." But in that case the car owner was standing by the open car door with a friend with the ignition key in his possession waiting for an employee to come to drive him away: he was not in charge. Nor was an insensible drunk in the back of an immobilised car: *Dean* v. *Wishart*, 1952 J.C. 9; nor the owner of a car sitting in the front passenger seat, his wife holding an expired provisional licence, occupying the driving seat with the engine running: *Winter* v. *Morrison*, 1954 J.C.7; nor an accused slumped over the driving wheel with no licence or insurance while his companion occupied the front passenger seat with licence, insurance and ignition keys: *Fisher* v. *Kearton* [1964] Crim. L.R. 470 (D.C.). See also *MacDonald* v. *Bain*, 1954 S.L.T. (Sh. Ct.) 30, *MacDonald* v. *MacDonald* (1955) 71 Sh. Ct. Reps. 17; *MacDonald* v. *Kubirdas*, 1955 S.L.T. (Sh. Ct.) 50 and *Farrell* v. *Campbell*, 1959 S.L.T. (Sh. Ct.) 43.

On the other hand a person in possession of ignition keys looking for his car and arrested before he could enter it was held to be in charge: *Leach* v. *Evans* [1952] 2 All E.R. 264, as was the supervisor of a learner driver: *Clark* v. *Clark*, 1950 S.L.T. (Sh. Ct.) 68, a taxi-driver awaiting a tow in his broken-down taxi: *MacDonald* v. *Crawford*, 1952 S.L.T. (Sh. Ct.) 92, and a motor cyclist whose companions were arranging that someone else should ride his cycle; *Haines* v. *Roberts* [1953] 1 All E.R. 344. It may be a nice question when a person ceased to be in charge. In *Ellis* v. *Smith* [1962] 3 All E.R. 954 a bus driver who went off duty leaving his bus on the road was held still in charge until he handed over to another driver. It would seem however that there may be circumstances where a driver has abandoned his vehicle so decisively that he could no longer be held in charge. What is clear is that mere delivery of the ignition key to a drinking companion will avail nothing: *Thaw* v. *Segar*, 1962 S.L.T. (Sh. Ct.) 63.

It is clear from *Northfield* v. *Pinder* [1969] 2 W.L.R. 50 that evidence in support of the statutory defence to the in-charge variant of the prescribed level offence must go so far as to show on a balance of probabilities that there is no likelihood of the accused driving so long as his excess alcohol level persists. This may be difficult to establish since the presence of excess alcohol can only be revealed by repeated checks. Section 4 of the Road Safety Act 1967 provides the police with power to detain a person from whom laboratory specimens have been requisitioned until such time as they have been satisfied from breath tests that the blood-alcohol level has dropped below the limit. As the rule is not mandatory in suitable cases an accused may be released leaving his vehicle behind. A person arrested for the prescribed-level offence, unlike any other, does not apparently have to be brought immediately before a magistrate.

The practical feature of the in-charge offences which distinguishes them from the principal offences is that though disqualification may be ordered it is not a mandatory punishment.

THE IMPAIRMENT OFFENCE

Having established that the accused drove a vehicle on a road or public place the central nature of the impairment offence must be examined—driving or attempting to drive while a person's ability to drive properly is for the time being impaired by drink or drugs. The offence is one, but may be committed by indulgence in drink or in drugs or of course in both. It is not therefore bad for duplicity: *Thomson* v. *Knights* [1947] K.B. 336.

The offence is committed, it is to be observed, at the moment of driving. This introduces a problem since the evidence of impairment must be related to the material time. Frequently that evidence takes the form of observation of the driving. Evidence of driving observed three miles away was acceptable in *R*. v. *Burdon* (1927) 20 Cr. App. R. 80, but the fact of unexceptionable driving over as little as 200 yards was not sufficient to rebut medical evidence of unfitness in *Murray* v. *Muir*, 1949 J.C. 127. It is perhaps more common to find a vehicle driven by one whose ability is impaired by drink to be travelling slowly rather than too fast. Sometimes the observer describes the vehicle as zig-zagging in the road almost as one might imagine a drunk pedestrian to walk. Failure to relate to traffic conditions, driving too near the kerb, negotiating corners awkwardly, responding slowly or not at all to signs and signals may suggest impairment, but may of course also be attributable to other causes. Linked with other evidence these matters may be of importance in particular because they are suggestive of impairment at the material time.

A question is sometimes raised whether incidental evidence of drink is admissible in cases of other driving offences such as causing death by dangerous driving where no drink-driving offence applies. In *R*. v. *Norrington* [1960] Crim. L.R. 432 evidence of urine-alcohol tests was admitted in such a case, while in *R*. v. *Sibley* [1962] Crim. L.R. 397 evidence of visits to public houses was allowed to stand, but it had not been suggested that drink was the cause of the accident. No doubt the factors to be regarded would be the relevance and materiality of the evidence, fair notice and absence of prejudice to the accused. It is probably better practice, however, to avoid evidence of drink in such cases altogether.

The attention of the police may in impairment cases be drawn to a vehicle by an informant, by its involvement in an accident or by the way in which it is driven. Police evidence is generally given of the encounter between the police and the driver, often of their request that he should leave his vehicle, produce his licence, and accompany them under arrest to the police station. The power of arrest without warrant (under the Road Traffic Act 1960, s. 6(4)) may be exercised if the police reasonably conclude from his conduct or condition or from other evidence that the driver is unfit to drive, even though this may later prove not to be so: *Wiltshire* v. *Barrett* [1966] 1 Q.B. 312. Clearly, weight may be attached to the driver's behaviour and appearance, but such facts as that his breath "smells strongly of drink" and that he fumbles in producing his licence from his pocket, though almost invariably given, seem in themselves virtually worthless. In America sound films of the accused's behaviour have been used as evidence (*Sweeny*). The question of arrest is dealt with more fully in Chapter 12.

At the police station the accused person is normally cautioned and charged with the offence and is always entitled to an interview in private with his solicitor—Summary Jurisdiction (Scotland) Act 1954, s. 12. In England he may be admitted to bail by the station officer—Magistrates' Courts Act 1952, s. 38; in Scotland this can in practice only be done by the Sheriff after committal: Bail (Scotland) Act 1888, s. 2, though application may be and normally is made at the accused's first appearance in court: Criminal Procedure (Scotland) Act 1887, s. 18. He must be brought before the court at the earliest practicable time, and should not be detained overnight uncharged: *R.* v. *Morgan* [1961] Crim. L.R. 538. Where it is inconvenient to have the accused brought before the court the following day he may instead be released and ordained to appear at a fixed date.

Where he is to be medically examined (and this should follow in every case to exclude illness or injury and to satisfy the police of his fitness to be detained) the accused must be informed by the police doctor of what is proposed, and his consent sought and obtained. The fact of consent to examination need not be corroborated, even in Scotland: *Farrell* v. *Concannon*, 1957 J.C. 12. The accused may not be medically examined against his will, or at least without his concurrence: *Taylor* v. *Irvine*, 1958 S.L.T. (Notes) 15 though where he declines his conduct may and should be circumspectly observed. It is proper for the doctor to inform the accused that failing consent his conduct will be observed: *Wishart* v. *Fenwick*, 1968 S.L.T. 263. The accused must be permitted to request the attendance of a doctor of his own choosing, though it is unusual for such a request to meet with enthusiastic response from medical men. In Scotland the law requires the police doctor's examination to be carried out privately and without questions directed to elicit information bearing on the accused's guilt: *Reid* v. *Nixon*; *Dumigan* v. *Brown*, 1948 J.C. 68; *Harris* v. *Adair*, 1947 J.C. 116: but in England it is more usual for the police to be present though preferably out of earshot: *The Drinking Driver*, B.M.A. 1965. The results of medical examination carried out before caution and charges are inadmissible in Scotland: *Gallacher* v. *H. M. Advocate*, 1963 S.L.T. 217 and have been excluded from evidence in England where the accused was not told of his right to refuse: *R.* v. *Urech* [1962] C.L.Y. 587 or where he gave consent on the understanding that the examination was purely to eliminate the possibility of illness or injury: *R.* v. *Payne* [1963] 1 All E.R. 848. Consent obtained through a mistaken belief that the proceedings were regular might well be held to be ineffective should the arrest for example have been made without the necessary circumstances warranting it.

Something has been made of the fact that in England the evidence of the police doctor is to be regarded as "that of a professional man giving independent expert evidence with no other desire than to assist the court"—*R.* v. *Nowell* [1948] 1 All E.R. 794: "an impartial witness"—*The Drinking Driver*, B.M.A. 1965: while in Scotland he is simply a prosecution witness and so (as was conceded in *Reid* v. *Nixon, supra*) "the hand of the police." The medical evidence in such a case is to be regarded in the same way as that of any other independent witness: *R.* v. *Lanfear* [1968] 2 Q.B. 77 (disapproving the statement of law in Archbold 36th Ed. para. 2849, which could give a false impression of the weight to be attached to the evidence) and doctors involved on whichever side will for professional reasons avoid an unduly partisan approach.

The question of the expert nature of the doctor's evidence is discussed in Chapter 14.

The layman may give evidence as to whether the accused has

been drinking, but the question whether he is fit to drive, being the issue before the court, is not a proper one even for an experienced driver: *R. v. Davies* [1962] 3 All E.R. 97; though where in substance the evidence amounts to the observation of an experienced driver it may be permitted as in *R. v. Neal* [1962] Crim. L.R. 698. The police doctor's opinion, though dealing with fitness to drive, is not initially related directly to the material time of driving and is rarely attacked on the ground that it tends to usurp the issue before the court. Should the accused have managed to consume additional drink after the material time it might be impossible for the court to decide what his condition was before having taken the drink, though the circumstances of the additional drinking could themselves be suggestive of guilt. Where a driver whose car had scraped a building returned home, a distance of only 300 yards, consumed two large whiskies, was called on to provide a breath specimen, was arrested and taken to the police station where a blood test showed more than the prescribed alcohol level, and was convicted of the prescribed-level offence, the court held on appeal that it had been wrong to disregard the drink consumed after driving, and the conviction was quashed: *Wood* v. *Brown,* 1969 S.L.T. (Notes) 65. It is often forgotten that drugs too may be consumed after the impairment offence with a consequential effect upon the accused's condition. The quantity of drink consumed is frequently proved by the evidence of the accused or by that of his companions, often with wildly optimistic estimates of its lack of effect. The fact of having taken drink or drugs is essential to the impairment offence. It is of course possible to be affected by drugs which have not been "consumed," and it seems that the expression "through drink or drugs" is deliberately a wide one. A person who had taken drink but whose ability to drive was impaired by illness would not necessarily be guilty of an offence. There have been cases of drivers claiming to be affected by the fumes of distilleries, (but see *supra,* p. 21) and unwitting carbon monoxide poisoning from leaking exhaust fumes can simulate the effects of drink, though this can easily be revealed by an immediate blood test (pp. 110-111). In this connection "drug" means any medicine given to cure, alleviate or assist an ailing body and includes insulin: *Armstrong* v. *Clark* [1957] 2 Q.B. 391 (*cf.* p. 103). Lord Chief Justice Goddard in that case expressed the cautious opinion that the term "drink" means alcoholic drink. A diabetic who due to an unforeseen shift of body metabolism becomes subject to a hypoglycaemic episode may be acquitted of the impairment offence—*Watmore* v. *Jenkins* [1962] 2 Q.B. 572, though he might be unwise to expect to fare so well on a second occasion. The offence for a driver lies not in taking the drink or drugs nor even in having taken them, but in the impairment of proper driving ability to which this may later lead. As indicated in the earlier chapters of this book there may well be a lapse of time before the offence is committed. That is to say a driver may set out able to drive properly but in the course of his journey the effect of drink or drugs may begin to make itself felt on his driving ability. In such a situation the offence is committed as soon as driving ability begins to be affected. Even a driver whose original impairment arises in a way not punishable within the scope of the law, and who persists in driving after realising its effects, risks successful prosecution.

A person arrested and charged with the impairment offence must be given the opportunity at the police station to provide a specimen of breath for a breath test, but it seems that failure to comply carries in this case no penal consequences. These attach only to failure to comply when requested to do so under section 2 of the 1967 Act. Such a request made to a person arrested for the impairment offence might therefore generally be refused, for should the breath test prove positive a person arrested and charged with the impairment offence would more likely be subjected to the demand for a blood or urine specimen which may be sought on his arrest and which could provide evidence in support of his alleged impaired driving ability. Whether a person arrested originally under the 1967 Act from whom a breath test was required, and who was subsequently proceeded against for the impairment offence could be convicted of failure to give a breath specimen, is uncertain. Failure to supply a specimen for laboratory tests in connection with the impairment charge is punishable as in the case of the prescribed alcohol level offence.

The provisions of section 2 of the Road Traffic Act 1962 are applied to impairment offence cases so that the court may have regard to evidence of the alcohol content of blood or urine and may take the accused's refusal to provide blood or urine (but not breath) specimens when requested by a constable, unless there is reasonable cause for his refusal, as supporting the prosecution case or rebutting the defence. To this end the provisions regarding proof by certificate are also to apply: *cf.* p. 156.

In all questions of incompetent or inadmissible evidence the importance of raising objection at the time must be kept in mind. For the consequences of failure to do so in England see *Newark*; and for the peremptory Scots rule see Summary Jurisdiction (Scotland) Act 1954, s. 73(1), and *Reid* v. *Nixon,* 1948 J.C. at p. 73

The standard of unfitness

It is curious that despite much criticism of the terms of the impairment offence there has been no close judicial examination of its meaning either in its original or in its amended form. It is arguable that the amendment made in 1962 brought about no significant improvement in its clarity (Smith J. C.). No doubt impairment means impairment in however small a degree, and ability to drive, though necessarily subjective, is an intelligible matter for enquiry, but ability to drive properly seems to imply reference to an objective standard of proper driving which is still remarkably elusive to define. It is sometimes argued that any observable physical consequence of taking alcohol, such as nystagmus, must imply impairment of driving ability, but rarely if ever is evidence given that nystagmus is correlated with diminished driving ability, let alone with a diminution which falls below the standard of proper driving. Since it must be accepted that driving ability varies from person to person, and even perhaps in the same person on different occasions, it seems unlikely that there can be a truly objective and fixed standard of proper driving ability. Does it therefore mean that impairment of a person's ability to drive as well as that person would otherwise have driven is the mischief aimed at by the statutory offence? What, if any, are the tolerances allowed? The absence of answers to these questions necessarily gives scope for the defence in borderline cases, though it may well avail nothing in the grosser cases where control of the vehicle is almost absent. This unsatisfactory situation also led to much criticism of the law and strengthened the demand for the creation of the complementary prescribed alcohol level offence.

THE PRESCRIBED ALCOHOL LEVEL OFFENCE

The prescribed alcohol level offence was created by the Road Safety Act 1967, s. 1, which came into operation on October 9, 1967. This provided that if a person drives or attempts to drive a vehicle on a road or other public place having consumed alcohol in such a quantity that the proportion thereof in his blood, as ascertained from a laboratory test, exceeds the prescribed limit at the time he provides a specimen of blood or urine for the purpose of that test, he shall be guilty of an offence. The Act can only be brought into operation after the application of a preliminary screening breath test which may be applied only in certain defined circumstances. Only those who fail the screening test or refuse it without reasonable excuse may be proceeded against. The others are discharged by compliance: *Brennan* v. *Farrell* [1969], Crim. L.R. 494, *per* Lord Walker. The Act then provides for those who fail or refuse the screening test to be required to supply blood or urine specimens for laboratory testing on pain of punishment for refusal if they will not or do not comply. An accused who has failed or refused to supply a breath test, or who has failed or refused to supply either blood or urine in response to a requirement under the Act, is treated in substantially the same way as a person who has been convicted of the prescribed level offence. See the chapter dealing with penalties at p. 149.

The prescribed-level offence concerns blood alcohol only and has no relevance to the misuse of drugs despite the rubric of the Act which reads "An Act to make further provision with respect to persons driving or being in charge of motor vehicles after consuming alcohol or taking drugs. . . ." The inclusion of the reference to drugs is necessary because amongst other things the Act amends the previous law of driving while impaired through drink or drugs. Although the language of section 1 seems to create an offence of strict liability applicable to all who show a blood alcohol level above that prescribed, the use of the expression "having consumed alcohol" seems inadequate to cover those to whom it has unknowingly been administered and it is probable that the voluntary act of the accused in consuming the alcohol would be necessary for conviction.

The evidential restriction of the offence to alcohol level "as ascertained from a laboratory test" seems to mean that the offence can be proved in one way only, and therefore a conviction is vulnerable to any substantial doubt raised in regard to the laboratory tests. As will be explained, the procedures preliminary to demanding screening breath tests are as strictly dependent upon compliance with the statutory provisions as are the breath tests themselves, and it follows that any failure or irregularity may be fatal to conviction. Each step in the procedure is justified only if every preceding step has been properly carried out: *cf. Scott* v. *Baker* [1969] 1 Q.B. 659. For these reasons the prescribed level offence, which set out to be precise and unchallengeable, has turned out in practice to be just as open to attack as the looser and vaguer impairment offence ever was.

It is important to keep in mind that the prescribed level offence has nothing to do with actual impairment. It is possible that the most habituated of drinkers could tolerate 80 milligrammes of alcohol per 100 millilitres of blood without adverse effect on driving ability, although most people suffer at least some impairment at that level. Conversely a driver may be obviously impaired and yet may not have attained the prescribed level.

The Act makes great demands upon and requires surrender of some of the cherished privileges of the public. Thus it allows the police wide powers to set enquiries in motion, demands submission to rather humiliating tests, virtually forces or at least induces the accused to supply evidence upon which alone he may be convicted, and permits the luxury of non-co-operation only in exchange for conviction of an offence virtually identical with that in regard to which co-operation was refused. These inroads upon the liberties of the subject could only be justified if they were acceptable to the public and resulted in a marked diminution in the toll of road accidents. The indications so far are that the Act is operating moderately well, if unevenly, and that it has produced a reduction in casualties, though the originally sharp public reaction to screening breath tests may be wearing off. The Act seems for the moment to have proved socially acceptable, a situation which might be unlikely to continue if the Minister of Transport exercised his power to lower the prescribed limit. There are however some who consider the present limit too high; and the view has been expressed that no limit is better than one which is too high (*Havard* 1963).

The screening breath test

Section 2 permits a constable in uniform to require any person driving or attempting to drive a vehicle to provide a specimen of breath for a breath test on the road or nearby (not it seems at a police station) if, but only if, he has reasonable cause either to suspect him (a) of having alcohol in his body, (b) of having been involved in an accident, or (c) of having committed a moving traffic offence; in the last case however the requirement must be made as soon as reasonably practicable after the traffic offence has occurred. It may of course be a continuing offence as in *R.* v. *Price*

[1968] 1 W.L.R. 1853. There is no set form of words in which the demand for a breath specimen must be made: *R.* v. *Clarke* [1969] 1 W.L.R. 1109.

The Act's requirement that the breath test can be applied only by a constable raises the question whether other ranks in the police service are excluded: the Act gives no definition. In practice much of the work is carried out by the police sergeant in charge at the station to which the accused is likely to be taken, and it would be strange indeed if it were intended that he should not be permitted to administer the terms of the Act. There is also the insistence that the constable should be in uniform. Although this is obviously a safeguard for the public, it is open to construction. The fact that the constable was in uniform should be proved. In *Morton* v. *Young* (Stranraer Sheriff Court: May 21, 1969) an accused charged with failing to give a breath specimen was acquitted because no evidence had been given that the two patrol policemen who stopped him and requested a breath test were in uniform. It is likely that most courts would be prepared to take judicial knowledge of the fact that police officers on patrol duties normally wear uniforms. This would still leave the question of what constitutes a uniform. In *Wood* v. *Brown,* 1969 S.L.T. (Notes) 65 the court drew such an inference.

The construction of the term "nearby" was considered in *Donegani* v. *Ward* [1969] 1 W.L.R. 1502, where it was held that what was "nearby" was a question of fact for the court to decide, but it was conceded that 160 yards distance could, in some circumstances, be considered to be "nearby": and see *Arnold* v. *Kingston-upon-Hull Chief Constable* [1969] 1 W.L.R. 1499.

What amounts to reasonable cause to suspect that a person has alcohol in the body must be a matter of particular circumstances, a few examples of which are given by *Seago* at [1969] Crim. L.R. 293. The suspicion need not be aroused during the period of actual driving: *Pinner* v. *Everett* [1969] 1, W.L.R. 1266, although it would have to be closely related to it. It is sufficient that the driver's breath smells of drink; and it may be a reasonable inference in regard to any person leaving licensed premises, particularly at closing time, or driving with a bottle of liquor on display in the vehicle. It does not matter what the objective truth happened to be, unknown to the police constable, at the time: what matters is whether the constable had reasonable cause to suspect the presence of alcohol: *McNichol* v. *Peters,* 1969 S.L.T. 261. Since a constable in uniform has power under section 223 of the Road Traffic Act 1960 to stop the driver of any vehicle on a road, it is clear that there is not in practice much difference between the original random testing proposed in the White Paper and the limited power to call for a screening breath test as it has turned out in the Road Safety Act 1967.

The interpretation of requiring a breath test from "a person driving or attempting to drive" must obviously be given some latitude. The Act could hardly be held to demand dangerous practices involving moving vehicles. The courts have however been unwilling to extend the interpretation of driving beyond the common sense notion of the person who is found in the driving seat when the car is stationary, or who leaves the car for a purpose connected with driving and can still be reasonably termed "driver": *R.* v. *Price* [1968] 1 W.L.R. 1853; *Pinner* v. *Everett,* p. 133 *supra,* as can a person who after driving remained slumped at the wheel of his car apparently unconscious for twenty minutes; *Purvis* v. *Hogg* (1969) 113 S.J. 388. But a request to a person who has parked his car, locked it and is about to enter a house (having apparently completed his journey) comes too late: *Campbell* v. *Tormey* [1969] Crim. L.R. 150, *R.* v. *Wall* [1969] I W.L.R. 400. A driver who had reached home and was taking drink there was however apparently treated as driving in *Wood* v. *Brown,* 1969 S.L.T. (Notes) 65. But a temporary absence from the car for example, to visit a toilet, will not terminate driving for this purpose: *R.* v. *Price, supra.* There may be some awkwardness in adopting this extended interpretation of driving to other parts of the Act. It does not fit, for example, in section 2(2). It is imported also into the impairment offence as, for example, by section 3(3) and (4)(c) of the Road Safety Act 1967 (dealing with failure to provide a laboratory specimen while driving at the time of arrest for the impairment offence). In Scotland the fact of driving will require corroboration.

Although it is an offence to be in charge of a vehicle with more than the prescribed blood-alcohol level, a breath test cannot be demanded from a person who is in charge though not driving or attempting to drive, unless an accident has occurred in circumstances in which it is reasonable to believe that the person in charge had been driving. A constable coming upon a person sitting quietly in a car at the roadside drinking from a bottle would be unable to proceed against that person under the Road Safety Act 1967 unless and until the driver attempted to drive away. The purpose of this apparent omission from the Act is said to be to provide an incentive for drivers who recognise that they have become affected by drink to pull off the road. A government pamphlet *The New Law on Drinking and Driving—the Facts you should Know* has been criticised for its too liberal statement of the law. Since such persons are still liable to prosecution for the impairment offence it is doubtful if the concession serves much practical purpose, and drivers who have relied upon the pamphlet have not always found its advice helpful.

If an accident has occurred the person whom a constable reasonably believes to have been the driver may be required to give a breath test either on the spot or (in case the equipment is not to hand) at a specified police station. The term "accident" is undefined by the Act and will obviously require consideration. If the driver is a patient in hospital or is being treated as an outpatient the breath test can only be given if (a) the intention to demand it is notified to the doctor in immediate charge of the patient and (b) that doctor does not raise the objection that the demand for the breath test, or the test itself, would be prejudicial to the proper care or treatment of the patient. Whether a doctor's surgery, a nursing home, a private clinic or a health centre would qualify as a "hospital" remains to be seen. The doctor's concurrence in the breath test being administered at the hospital may be proved at second hand: *R.* v. *Chapman* [1969] 2 W.L.R. 1004.

A breath test is defined in section 7(1) as a test for the purpose of obtaining an indication of the proportion of alcohol in a person's blood carried out by means of a device of a type approved for the purpose by the Secretary of State on a specimen of breath provided by that person. The question of approval, discussed later at p. 139 is one which has given a great deal of trouble. This definition of a breath test together with the evidential restriction upon the method of proof of the prescribed level offence have the effect of rendering evidence of the Alcotest result incompetent in support of the prescribed level offence itself. Failure to provide a breath specimen includes refusal to do so, but probably excludes circumstances which are beyond the driver's control such as defective equipment or absence of equipment: *Hoyle* v. *Walsh* [1969] 1 All E.R. 39. Where the driver has taken no exception at the time to reasonable police instructions, the procedure in Scotland is acceptable: *McLeod* v. *Milligan*: *Farrel* v. *Coakley* (1969) 14 J.L.S. 253.

In England failure to observe the Alcotest instructions may vitiate the procedure: *Webber* v. *Carey* [1969] 1 W.L.R. 1351 (See *Adams J. N.*). Providing a specimen of breath means providing a specimen in sufficient quantity to enable a breath test to be carried out—section 7(3)—the only statutory provision regarding the quantity of breath demanded. The Act makes no provision as to the quality of breath, and it has been held in Scotland that where the bag attached to the device was inflated with two breaths this compliance with the requirement to provide a specimen satisfied the Act and discharged the accused's obligation: *Brennan* v. *Farrell* [1969] Crim. L.R. 494. Since there is no requirement in the Act as to the manner in which the breath specimen is to be given it is not possible to enforce the directions which accompany the breath test device and with which the police have been accustomed to require compliance as to providing the breath with one deep exhalation and after a period to allow for the disappearance of traces of mouth alcohol. The result of this case is that it is not possible to be certain that borderline cases can be detected by the Alcotest device. In England however the opposite result has been reached in the case of *R.* v. *Chapman* [1969] 2 W.L.R. 1004 where it was held that approval of the Secretary of State of the breath test device included approval of the instructions which accompany it, including the direction that the device should be inflated in a single breath. This discrepancy of interpretation appears to be the first major matter in which the English and Scottish courts have reached a substantially different interpretation of an important provision of the Road Safety Act. The English judgment is however less than positive in its finding regarding the Secretary of State's approval which "no doubt embraced the instructions of how the test is to be taken": *per* Fenton Atkinson L.J. at p. 1007. If the device fails, a second test may be administered: *McKay* v. *MacLeod* (unreported). A driver who drove off because equipment was not to hand was held to have failed to take the test: *R.* v. *Clarke* [1969] Crim. L.R. 441.

A person who without reasonable excuse fails to provide a specimen of breath shall be liable on summary conviction to a fine not exceeding £50—the first instalment of the punishment which non-co-operation under the Act is likely to involve. The Act confers no right upon the accused to receive a specimen of breath for his own use.

The demand for a breath specimen under the Road Safety Act

1967 is always mandatory, and it is necessary for the constable to make this clear to the driver in peremptory terms: *Brown* v. *Teasdale*, 1968 S.L.T. (Sh. Ct.) 67. But there are no set words which must be used: *R.* v. *Clarke* [1969] 1 W.L.R. 1109.

It is clear that the power conferred upon the police by section 2 to require a breath test in a particular case may be exercised only once, unless fresh circumstances arise to justify a new request being made of a driver. If therefore an accused fairly carries through the procedure, he has done what the Act requires of him. There have however been cases in which for one reason or another the original procedure gets off to a false start, or the device becomes or is discovered to have been unserviceable. It is then a question whether what has transpired can be regarded as a fair compliance with the requirements of the Act. For example when the Alcotest bag burst it was held that the accused had fairly played his part and the police were not entitled to demand a second test: *Hawthorn* v. *Swan*, Falkirk Sheriff Court, May 29, 1969. Had the defect occurred because of some deliberate act on the part of the accused this could have resulted otherwise, and there have been many cases where the accused has protested that he is unable to blow through the device or that he cannot fully inflate the plastic bag, and most of these have been resolved as failures or refusals to provide a sample. A person who cannot render a specimen of breath because of a defect in the device has not discharged the obligation imposed by the Act and may be asked to try again on a fresh device. What is reasonable excuse for a refusal to provide a breath test will be for the courts to decide, and would seem to be a question of fact: *Leck* v. *Epsom Rural D.C.* [1922] 1 K.B. 383. Perhaps the fact that the accused suffered from a critical lung complaint, from an uncorrected hernia, or from chronic asthma would serve, though the view has been expressed (*Havard* 1967) that asthmatics are used to breathing out against resistance and should be exceptionally proficient at inflating the bag. Certainly the disability would have to be backed up by medical evidence. The burden is on the prosecution to disprove reasonable excuse: *R.* v. *Clarke* [1969] 1 W.L.R. 1109. Being too drunk to inflate the bag is obviously no excuse: *R.* v. *Chapman* [1969] 2 W.L.R. 1004. Professional glass blowers may find the Act not unduly burdensome to them.

It is one of the most oppressive features of the Road Safety Act 1967 that while it is no offence to refuse to supply a breath specimen where reasonable excuse exists, the accused who wishes to vindicate himself may have to submit to arrest and the indignity of police procedure followed by a court hearing before he can expect to do so.

The White Paper described the first breath test as "the roadside screening test" and section 2(1) contemplates the breath test being performed on the road or nearby, and, where it is required because of a suspected traffic offence, as soon as reasonably practical after commission (this must mean the suspected commission) of the offence. The latitude of proximity of time and place permitted by this section has yet to be judicially determined.

A person who fails to provide a breath test when requested to do so under the Act may be arrested by the constable without warrant if the constable suspects that he has alcohol in his body, though not so long as he is an in- or out-patient at a hospital. A person who fails to provide a breath test when arrested and taken to the police station is to be given another opportunity to provide a breath test there. No doubt if he does so the earlier refusal would be disregarded, though this need not be so even when the second offer of a breath test is taken up and results in an indication that his blood alcohol does not exceed the prescribed limit. To found a conviction under section 2(3) of the Road Safety Act 1967 the refusal of the breath test will have to be corroborated: cf. *Farrell* v. *Concannon*, 1957 J.C. 12. The police, in arresting a person failing or refusing to provide a breath specimen, have no concern with reasonable excuse for not so providing. This is a matter entirely for the court. Absence of alcohol is not reasonable excuse: *McNicol* v. *Peters*, 1969 S.L.T. 261.

The conduct of the breath test (described *supra,* at pp. 78 and 132) is in the hands of the police constable. Where in the constable's judgment the Alcotest indicates that the proportion of alcohol in the accused's blood exceeds the prescribed limit (*i.e.* where the granules turn green beyond the yellow line) the constable may arrest the accused without warrant and proceed to the second stage at which laboratory tests are demanded. Where the breath test is properly carried out and the granules do not turn green beyond the line, the accused cannot be further proceeded against under the Road Safety Act and must be released or dealt with as for the impairment offence. The interpretation of the Alcotest in borderline cases is not easy and could perhaps be variously assessed. Since the matter is for the police constable it may be that the accused is not entitled to examine the Alcotest device, though in most cases he is allowed to do so. In some courts the device is produced as an exhibit at the trial, though the reading on the tube may long since have deteriorated, and for this reason —among others—some police forces routinely destroy the tubes, a procedure approved in *Miller* v. *Howe* [1969] 1 W.L.R. 1510. Although the device is of little assistance after an interval for determining whether or not it registered a positive reading, the accused may have an interest to show whether it was obstructed or defective, and there is much to be said for retaining the device until the hearing of the case. Although English law no longer insists on production of the best evidence where physical objects are concerned (Cross, *Evidence*, 3rd ed., p. 11), the Scottish courts still require that such an object should be produced where it is practicable and convenient to do so (Walker & Walker, *Law of Evidence*, p. 445).

Much difficulty arose in the early days of the operation of the Road Safety Act through the slowness of the authorities in approving the device to be used by the police, and several cases in which approval had not been adequately proved were dismissed. If the matter is taken up by the defence the fact of approval of the device used has to to be competently proved in court: *Scott* v. *Baker* [1969] 1 Q.B. 659. It is insufficient to rely upon the label on the box in which the Alcotest device is supplied: *R.* v. *Gwilliam* [1968] 1 W.L.R. 1839 but *cf. Miller* v. *Howe* [1969] 1 W.L.R. 1510. The evidence of the official who gave approval acting on behalf of the Secretary of State is adequate: *R.* v. *Skinner* [1968] 2 Q.B. 700 or the evidence of an official having knowledge of that approval: *R.* v. *Holt* [1968] I W.L.R. 1942 or, in England, proof under the Documentary Evidence Act 1868 as amended by production of a Stationary Office copy of the order even though it does not have the status of a statutory instrument: *R.* v. *Clarke* [1969] 2 W.L.R. 505 (but *cf. R.* v. *Storer* [1969] Crim. L.R. 204). In *R.* v. *Chapman* [1969] 2 W.L.R. 1004, apparently contradicting the decision in *Brennan* v. *Farrell* [1969] Crim. L.R. 494, the Court of Appeal held that the Secretary of State's approval included approval of the instructions for use of the breath test device, and was evidence of the correctness of the direction that the device should be inflated in a single breath. In Scotland the production of even a copy letter from the Department concerned to the manufacturers suffices: *Hunter* v. *Herron,*

1969 S.L.T. (Notes) 54. But see *Lockhart* v. *Coakley*, 1969 S.L.T. (Sh. Ct.) 26.

The Breath Test Device (Approval) (No. 1) Order 1969 made on February 9, 1968, approves the Alcotest device used in England and Wales, the No. 2 Order approves the same device issued to members of the provost staff; and the order applicable to Scotland is The Breath Test Device (Approval) (Scotland) Order 1968 made on December 16, 1968. Proof of the approval order avails nothing in a case occurring before the commencement date of the order: *Farrow* v. *Bosomworth* [1969] Crim. L.R. 320.

Laboratory tests

The second stage of the Road Safety Act procedure involves the requisition of specimens for laboratory tests on which alone the evidence of blood-alcohol level will be based. The material time so far as the prescribed level offence is concerned is the time of taking the specimens. Although the White Paper stated the intention to encourage blood rather than urine samples, no direct statutory preference is expressed, and even the *routine* requesting of blood first and urine as second choice is only implied by section 3(6) of the Act. (See also p. 33.)

A person arrested because of a positive breath test or a person who has refused to provide a specimen of breath for testing but whom a constable suspects of having alcohol in his body, while under arrest at a police station may be required by the constable to provide a specimen of blood or urine for laboratory testing—section 3. Such a person will already have had a further opportunity (other than the roadside test) to provide a breath test at the station in accordance with section 2(7), and this must be afforded if the subsequent procedure is to be regular: *R.* v. *Withecombe* [1969] 1 W.L.R. 84.

On requiring the accused person to provide a blood or urine specimen for laboratory testing the constable must warn him that failure to provide a specimen of blood or urine may make him liable to imprisonment, a fine and disqualification. So important is this warning rated that failure to administer the warning may lead to the court acquitting the accused, or dismissing the charge against him: section 3(10). When there has been a failure to deliver the warning the court will endeavour to find out whether the accused has been prejudiced: *R.* v. *Brush* [1968] 1 W.L.R. 1740 though it is hard to see what prejudice there could be. The request for a blood or urine specimen must be accompanied by an offer by the police to supply the accused with a part of the specimen or a separate specimen as explained in what follows.

The request must be made and the specimen taken at the police station: *Cruickshank* v. *Moncur,* (Ayr Sheriff Court, (1969) 14 J.L.S. 253).

A constable may also require an in-patient or an out-patient at a hospital under similar circumstances to supply such a specimen for laboratory tests but only where (*a*) the intention to demand it is notified to the doctor in immediate charge of the patient and (*b*) that doctor does not raise the objection that the demand for the specimen, the provision of the specimen itself, or the warning required as to the consequences of refusal would be prejudicial to the proper care or treatment of the patient.

Where the person from whom a specimen for laboratory tests is requisitioned elects to provide blood he must consent to the taking of the blood specimen by a doctor, and must actually furnish it, otherwise he will be treated as refusing to supply the specimen. The time of giving the specimen is the time of giving the blood sample, not the time of giving consent: section 7(2). It would seem therefore that a person who expresses willingness to supply a blood specimen and from whom the doctor fails for whatever reason to extract a specimen of blood is nevertheless treated as refusing to supply a specimen. This may be so expressed to encourage co-operation on the part of accused persons. As no guidance is given as to the size of the specimen which an accused must provide it would be difficult to fault a person who supplied any reasonable quantity. In one pair of cases it was held that a specimen means the whole contents of a syringe, part of which may properly be given to the accused. Whether the remainder is retained in one container or two is immaterial: *Kidd* v. *Kidd*; *Ley* v. *Donegani* [1969] 1 Q.B. 320. The Act goes on to imply that a blood specimen should normally be divided, a part being given to the accused for his own purposes. This is not directly enacted but the Road Safety Act, s. 3(8), provides that the Road Traffic Act 1962, s. 2, subs. (2) to (7), shall apply to the prescribed level offence as they apply to the impairment offence. The effect is, so far as blood specimens are concerned, that where the accused on being required to give a blood specimen asks to be supplied with a specimen, evidence of the alcohol content of the specimen will not be admitted as prosecution evidence unless, either the specimen taken was divided and a part given to the accused, or a second specimen taken at the same time is made available to the accused: *R.* v. *Sharp* (No. 2) [1968] Crim. L.R. 452. The further requirement is added that the constable demanding a blood specimen shall *offer* the accused either a part of that specimen or if it is impracticable to divide it, another specimen for his own use—subsections (4) and (5). This should be done before the accused leaves the police station and in any event within a reasonable time, as to which the court will judge having regard to possible prejudice from the delay —*R.* v. *Sharp* [1968] 2 Q.B. 564. The offer of a specimen or part thereof means the offer to supply, not the actual supply of the specimen: *Farrell* v. *Nivett,* 1967 S.L.T. 33. The offer must be express: *R.* v. *Roberts* (1964) 48 Cr. App. R. 300, and either simultaneous or proximate to the request: *R.* v. *Price* [1964] 2 Q.B. 76; *R.* v. *Mitten* [1966] 1 Q.B. 10. Should the blood sample be indivisible the accused must be informed: *R.* v. *MacNamara* [1966] 11 C.L. 263. The request lies with the constable, not with the doctor: *R.* v. *Lewis* (1964) 49 Cr. App. R. 26. Where the specimen is asked for and obtained by the doctor it seems that the statutory right to receive a part of the specimen does not apply; the evidence contained in a certificate following on such a specimen taken by a doctor was not rendered incompetent by the failure to offer a part to the accused: *R.* v. *Dooley* [1964] 1 W.L.R. 648. If the accused does not ask at the time to be given a specimen it does not seem to matter if the specimens are not divided, unless perhaps questions of fundamental fairness were called into play. It has been held however in a case in which the police found that one of the three parts into which the blood specimen had been divided had congealed, and the accused complained that his part was too small for analysis except by gas chromatography and in any event had also congealed, that the specimen provided for the accused under the 1962 Act had to be one capable of analysis, and one which congealed at once did not satisfy the Act: *Earl* v. *Roy* [1969] 1 W.L.R. 1050. In that case evidence of the difficulty of obtaining independent analysis by gas chromatography was given and apparently not challenged and there was some indication that the court would take that difficulty into account in deciding upon the sufficiency of the specimen afforded to the accused. See the letter on this subject at [1968] Crim. L.R. 55. It would however be strange if the courts were to require in all cases that specimens sufficient for macro-analysis should be provided. Where the defence produced the evidence of an analyst that he had been unable to analyse the specimen supplied to the accused the court considered the issue whether the prosecution had shown that they had satisfied the requirements of the Act and discharged the burden of proof laid upon them: *R.* v. *Nixon* (1969) 113 S.J. 388.

See also *Cronkshaw* v. *Rydeheard* (1969) 113 S.J. 673. The specimen should be in a suitable container, but failure to place the container in an envelope does not render the prosecution inadmissible: *Moore* v. *Wilkinson* [1969] Crim. L.R. 493.

The Act gives no guidance as to where the specimen should be extracted, but it has been held to be at the discretion of the doctor subject to the locus being one from which it is reasonable and safe to extract the specimen. (See p. 65.) A driver who insisted that blood should be taken from his big toe and nowhere else was held to be refusing to supply a specimen in circumstances in which the doctor was unprepared to take the specimen from the toe: *Solesbury* v. *Pugh* [1969] 1 W.L.R. 1114. Another who offered it only from his penis was acquitted on other grounds: *MacLeod* v. *Parker,* Edinburgh Sheriff Court; November 25, 1968. But it is possible that a driver might be well justified in offering blood from one arm rather than the other, perhaps because of an injury or skin disease.

Where the driver from whom a specimen for laboratory tests is requisitioned elects to provide urine there is no specific requirement that consent must be given, though some degrees of co-operation is obviously required. The specimen can and it seems must be taken by the police, modesty notwithstanding: *cf.* the case referred to at p. 75. The same oblique provisions are applied to the supplying of urine as to the provision of blood; that is to say that the accused may ask to be supplied with a urine specimen and if he does so at the time, the urine analysis will not be admitted as prosecution evidence unless the accused was supplied with a part of the specimen, or with a second specimen taken on the same occasion. With urine specimens this alternative might in the past have proved a feat impossible of performance, involving the accused in waiting until sufficient urine could be passed to enable two specimens of adequate size to be taken. Modern analytical techniques however require as little as perhaps a teaspoonful which would divide to give two or three specimens of sufficient size. Again, a constable on requiring urine specimens must *offer* to supply the accused with a part of the specimen—Road Traffic Act 1962, s. 2 (4) and (5) even where the opportunity has arisen only because the accused asked permission to urinate: *R.* v. *Roberts* (1964) 48 Cr. App. R. 300. The Road Safety Act however blandly assumes that urine specimens will be duplicated and that two will be provided within one hour, obviously in order to allow it to be checked that the elimination phase has been reached. Unfortunately this part of the Act is by no means clear and its only provision on this score is that a person shall not be treated as refusing to supply a specimen of blood or urine for laboratory tests unless (a) he is first requested to provide a specimen of blood, but refuses to do so, (b) he is then requested to provide two specimens of urine within one hour of the request, but fails to provide them within one hour or refuses at any time within the hour to provide them, and (c) he is again requested to provide a specimen of blood but refuses to do so. The Act goes on to provide (s. 3(7)) that the first specimen of urine so provided shall be "disregarded" (presumably for the purpose of evidence) either in connection with the impairment offence or with the prescribed level offence.

This is an unsatisfactory method of legislating, if the intention is that every case shall follow the procedure just outlined where specimens are demanded for laboratory testing. It is one thing to require that this procedure shall be followed in all cases and quite another to say, as the Road Safety Act says in section 3 subsections (6) and (7) that no one shall be treated as refusing the tests unless this procedure was applied. So far as the Act is concerned those cases in which no question of refusal is involved cannot be said to contravene the letter of the law, though they may offend against its spirit, if the procedure has not been in accordance with the subsections. The important consequence of this state of affairs is that in cases where no question of refusal of laboratory tests arises there is no operative statutory requirement that for urine sampling two specimens should have been given within the hour, and consequently no assurance that the specimen used was taken in the elimination phase.

Finally, it should be emphasised that the Road Safety Act 1967 does not specifically penalise an excessive urine-alcohol level in drivers. The offence described by section 1 is the offence of having at the time of providing the specimen an excessive proportion of blood alcohol as ascertained from a laboratory test. We have explained in the earlier chapters of this book that blood alcohol is the most direct index of the effect of alcohol upon the human body, whereas urine alcohol must be related to the blood-alcohol level by a simple calculation, since it represents not the current blood-alcohol level at the time of sampling but the average level over a period in the past. Section 7(4) does not grapple with this difficulty but merely sets out an equivalence for the critical levels in urine and in blood. Unfortunately the Act does not state, though it can be argued that it implies, that the laboratory analysis of urine specimens shall be deemed to represent the blood-alcohol level *at the time when the specimen was given*. This may not matter in cases which are clearly above the prescribed level, but seems to call for a further minor adjustment to relate the translated figure which must represent blood-alcohol prior to the taking of the specimen into the appropriate figure representing the level at the time of taking the specimen.

CHAPTER 12

ARREST

A CONSTABLE in uniform has power under section 6(4) of the Road Traffic Act 1960 to arrest without warrant a person committing the impairment offence, or a person in charge whilst impaired.

There is no power directly to arrest a person suspected of committing the prescribed level offence, nor the offence of being in charge while the blood-alcohol level exceeds the prescribed limit. As explained in the previous chapter the police must approach the prescribed level offence by way of a request for a breath test followed by the requirement of laboratory tests. Under the Road Safety Act 1967, s. 2(4), a constable in uniform may without warrant arrest a person who has provided a breath specimen which the constable judges to show a positive reading on the breath test device, unless that person should be a hospital patient. Under section 2(5) of the same Act a constable in uniform has power to arrest without warrant a person who fails or refuses to provide a breath specimen for a breath test, unless that person should be a hospital patient, provided the constable has reason to suspect that he has alcohol in his body. This power of arrest persists even if there has been reasonable excuse for the accused person to refuse the breath test.

As in any other case there is a duty to inform the arrested person of the reason for his arrest: *Christie* v. *Leachinsky* [1947] A.C. 573, *Reid* v. *Nixon*, 1948 J.C. 68. An arrest is not rendered unlawful merely because the accused person is subsequently released and not further proceed against: *Wiltshire* v. *Barrett* [1966] 1 Q.B. 312.

In England, to ask the driver to come to the police station, provided he submits and knows that he is under restraint, is enough to constitute arrest in a road traffic case: *Alderson* v. *Booth* [1969] 2 W.L.R. 1252. In that case the accused's disclaimer that he did not know he was under restraint was believed, so that there was no arrest, and the subsequent breath and blood test procedure was vitiated. Similarly in *Hawthorn* v. *Kilgannon* (Stirling Sheriff Court, June 2, 1969) a driver who was invited to go to the police station for breath and blood tests was acquitted on the ground that the proper foundation of arrest had not been established. The fact of arrest is of course by definition an integral part of the prescribed level offence.

In *Campbell* v. *Tormey* [1969] 1 All E.R. 961 it was said that the constable ought in every case to make clear whether he was exercising the powers of arrest under section 6(4) of the Road Traffic Act 1960 or under section 2(4) or (5) of the Road Safety Act 1967. In *R.* v. *Wall* [1969] 1 All E.R. 968 however the Court of Appeal retracted this judgment to some extent, and came down in favour of allowing those cases in which a breath test is followed by arrest to be treated in accordance with the procedure for the prescribed level offence, unless impairment is suspected, in which case the accused ought to be informed that he was *also* being arrested under section 6(4) of the Road Traffic Act 1960.

It is uncertain whether this tactical manoeuvre of keeping both options open will satisfy the stricter rules of Scots law which have hitherto required, in connection with the impairment offence at least, that the accused should be clearly informed at the outset of the exact grounds on which his arrest is based: *Reid* v. *Nixon*, 1948 J.C. 68; *Harris* v. *Adair*, 1947 J.C. 116. The procedure there laid down for the impairment offence in Scotland is almost as rigorous as the statutory code now provided by the Road Safety Act 1967 for the prescribed level offence. The Scottish procedure demands that (1) the accused should be cautioned and charged, (2) his consent to clinical examination must be obtained, (3) he should be informed of his right to independent medical assistance, (4) the clinical examination should be conducted in private, (5) there should be no interrogation on the merits by the police doctor, and (6) nothing inadvertently elicited by the police doctor must be communicated to the police. Failure to caution and charge the accused before the clinical examination will normally render the medical evidence inadmissible: *Gallacher* v. *H.M. Advocate*, 1963 S.L.T. 217.

The statutory application of the breath test and laboratory test sections of the Road Safety Act 1967 to persons arrested for the impairment offence, and the effect of sections 3 (8) and (9) (which import the provisions of the Road Traffic Act 1960, s. 2 (2) to (7)) point to an interlocking of the three Acts: *cf. Roberts* v. *Jones* [1969] Crim. L.R. 90. It is not surprising therefore that questions of interchangeability of charges under these Acts have been raised.

So far as the impairment offence is concerned a person is normally arrested under section 6(4) of the Road Traffic Act 1960, and this may be done if necessary at an interval after the discovery of his driving or being in charge. It seems therefore that a person first arrested under the provisions of section 2(4) of the Road Safety Act 1967 may, if the breath test indicates that his blood-alcohol has not reached the prescribed level, be re-arrested this time on the ground of suspected impairment. There is however something smacking of unfairness in a procedure whereby the prosecutor foreseeing failure raises a second charge in succession to the first on which he has become doubtful. Likewise there seems nothing to prevent a person arrested under section 2(5) of the Road Safety Act 1967 for failure to provide a breath specimen being subsequently re-arrested and charged with the impairment offence, though the normal routine would be to follow through the laboratory tests procedure.

Where a person is under arrest for the impairment offence and the police doctor after clinical examination is doubtful whether there is impairment, it is permissible for the accused to be charged with the prescribed alcohol level offence so long as the police have not departed from their intention to prosecute for the original offence: *Coneys* v. *Nicholson* [1969] Crim. L.R. 34. Whether or not this last qualification of not departing from their intention to prosecute is really essential is open to question: *Roberts* v. *Jones* [1969] Crim. L.R. 90. If however a driver arrested for the impairment offence were released because the charge was not proceeding, he could hardly qualify as a driver from whom a breath test could be requested under section 2(1) of the Road Safety Act 1967.

Some doubts were entertained in the case of *Campbell* v. *Tormey* [1969] 1 All E.R. 961 as to whether a person "under arrest" is in an identical position to a person "arrested", but this probably illusory refinement is not one with which it is necessary to deal.

CHAPTER 13

PENALTIES

THE IMPAIRMENT OFFENCE; THE PRESCRIBED ALCOHOL LEVEL OFFENCE

IN the case of either of these offences the maximum penalties are as follows:

(a) on conviction on indictment—fine or imprisonment not exceeding 2 years or both:

(b) on summary conviction—fine not exceeding £100 or imprisonment not exceeding 4 months or both, but in the case of a second or subsequent conviction a fine not exceeding £100 or imprisonment not exceeding 6 months or both.

In addition there is mandatory disqualification from holding a driving licence for not less than 12 months unless there are special reasons which the court think justify disqualification for a shorter period or not at all. On a subsequent conviction within 10 years the court shall disqualify for not less than 3 years unless there exist special reasons to disqualify for a shorter period or not at all. Disqualification may be imposed subject to the accused passing a further test and obtaining a certificate of competence to drive.

A person convicted of the impairment offence and subsequently of the prescribed alcohol level offence or vice versa may be treated as though his conviction of one were a conviction of the other offence and accorded the more severe penalty as a result.

Both offences qualify for inclusion among those subject to the "totting up" provisions set out in section 5(3) of the Road Traffic Act 1962.

Endorsement is mandatory in the case of either offence when disqualification is imposed. If disqualification is not imposed there need not be endorsement if the court is satisfied that there are special reasons for not endorsing. An endorsement may be removed after a period of 10 years has elapsed.

These rules are derived from the Road Traffic Act 1960, s. 6, the Road Traffic Act 1962, ss. 5, and 7 and the First Schedule, and from the Road Safety Act 1967, ss. 1 and 5.

THE "IN CHARGE" OFFENCES: ROAD TRAFFIC ACT 1960, s. 6(2); ROAD SAFETY ACT 1967, s. 1(2)

In the case of either of these offences the maximum penalties are as follows:

(a) on conviction on indictment—fine or imprisonment not exceeding 12 months or both;

(b) on summary conviction—fine not exceeding £100 or imprisonment not exceeding 4 months or both.

In addition there is power to disqualify from holding a licence but this is not mandatory. Disqualification may be imposed subject to the accused passing a further driving test and obtaining a certificate of competence to drive.

A person convicted of the section 6(2) offence and subsequently of the section 1(2) offence or vice versa may be treated as though his conviction of one were a conviction of the other offence and accorded the more severe penalty as a result.

Both offences qualify for inclusion among those subject to the "totting up" provisions set out in section 5(3) of the Road Traffic Act 1962.

Endorsement is mandatory in the case of either offence when disqualification is imposed. If disqualification is not imposed there need not be endorsement if the court is satisfied that there are special reasons for not endorsing.

An endorsement may be removed after a period of three years has elapsed.

These rules are derived from the Road Traffic Act, 1960, s. 6, the Road Traffic Act 1962, ss. 5 and 7 and the First Schedule, and the Road Safety Act 1967, ss. 1 and 5.

FAILURE TO PROVIDE A BREATH TEST

In the case of failure without reasonable excuse to provide a specimen of breath for a breath test at the roadside or nearby, or at a hospital, the maximum penalty on summary conviction is a fine not exceeding £50. There is no endorsement for a conviction of this offence, and it is not an offence which counts for the purposes of the "totting up" provisions.

Failure to provide a breath specimen of course results in arrest and the demand for a specimen of blood or urine for laboratory test with the prospect of punishment if these lead to conviction or in the event of non-compliance without reasonable excuse. It seems inequitable that where the laboratory tests reveal no offence and the accused is acquitted his conviction for failure to supply a breath specimen could still proceed.

These rules are derived from section 2 of the Road Safety Act 1967.

FAILURE TO PROVIDE A LABORATORY SPECIMEN

(a) Where a person is arrested for the impairment offence or for failure to provide a breath test.

In the case of such a person driving or attempting to drive at the time of arrest or when required to provide a breath specimen failure without reasonable cause to provide a laboratory specimen of blood or urine attracts the following maximum penalties; namely the penalties provided in the case of conviction for the impairment offence (see p. 149). The consequences in regard to disqualification, endorsement, and special reasons which apply to a conviction for the impairment offence apply also to convictions for this offence.

These rules are derived from section 3 of the Road Safety Act 1967 and the authorities specified at p. 150, above.

(b) A person "in charge" at the time of an accident; or a person "in charge" while his proper driving ability was impaired.

In such cases failure without reasonable excuse to provide a laboratory specimen of blood or urine attracts the following penalties, namely the penalties provided in the case of conviction for the "in charge" offences (see p. 150). The consequences in regard to disqualification, endorsement and special reasons which apply to a conviction for the "in charge" offences apply also to conviction for these offences.

These rules are derived from section 3 of the Road Safety Act 1967 and the authorities specified at p. 150, above.

It is to be noted that while there is no power to demand a breath test from a person "in charge" with more than the prescribed blood-alcohol level and so no power to require such a person to provide a specimen of blood or urine for a laboratory test under the Road Safety Act 1967, if treated as "in charge" whilst proper driving ability is impaired such a person may be required to provide a blood or urine specimen and the result of non-compliance without reasonable excuse would attract identical punishment to that which would have followed had there been power to demand the breath sample, though of course the standards of proof may be different.

"Special Reasons"

(a) In regard to disqualification.

"Special reasons" must be special to the offence and not to the offender, mitigating in character though not themselves amounting to a substantive defence, yet directly connected with the offence and such as may properly be taken into account by the court: *Whittall* v. *Kirby* [1947] K.B. 194; *R.* v. *Wickins* (1958) 42 Cr. App. R. 236; *R.* v. *Steel* [1968] Crim. L.R. 450. The rule in Scotland is similar though with a greater emphasis on the aspect of protecting public safety: *Adair* v. *Munn*, 1940 J.C. 69; *Irvine* v. *Pollock*, 1952 J.C. 51; *Farlie* v. *Hill*, 1944 J.C. 53; *Carnegie* v. *Clark*, 1947 J.C. 74. The special reasons must be proved by the accused in evidence: *Jones* v. *English* [1951] 2 All E.R. 853; *R.* v. *Lundt-Smith* [1964] 2 Q.B. 167. It is a question of law: *Knowler* v. *Rennison* [1947] K.B. 488. The reason should be put forward at the first hearing: *Hynd* v. *Clark*, 1954 S.L.T. 85. The court has no wider discretion in finding special reasons to reduce or avoid disqualification in connection with the prescribed level offence than it had under the impairment offence: *Herron* v. *McDonagh*, 1969 S.L.T. 2.

The administration of drugs without the driver's knowledge if not a substantive defence could amount to special reasons: *Whittall* v. *Kirby, supra.*; also the fact that a driver unknown to him suffered from diabetes so that a small quantity of beer produced an exceptional effect: *R.* v. *Wickins, supra*; an unwitting overdose of drugs: *Chapman* v. *O'Hagan* [1949] 2 All E.R. 690; a dose of amytal tablets taken without warning of their dangers: *R.* v. *Holt* [1962] Crim. L.R. 565; and a person taking drink after a severe electric shock: *R.* v. *Julien* [1966] Crim. L.R. 52. Likewise the combination of alcohol with inhalation of trichlorethylene fumes: *Brewer* v. *Metropolitan Police Commissioner* [1969] 1 W.L.R. 267. But different considerations can apply in cases involving the impairment offence and cases involving the prescribed alcohol level offence. In *R.* v. *Scott* [1969] 2 All E.R. 450 (C.A.) the taking of sleeping tablets when the driver had no idea of their adverse effect on alcohol in her blood was not regarded as special reason for not disqualifying on the prescribed alcohol level offence, though the question whether it might have been special reason in the impairment offence was reserved.

The situation outlined in the pamphlet *The New Law on Drinking & Driving* (see p. 135) covering unexpected medical emergency also qualifies: *Brown* v. *Dyerson* [1968] 3 W.L.R. 615.

The fact that the accused was tired, driving on an empty stomach or unwell and so excessively affected by a small quantity of drink has frequently been rejected as a special reason: *cf. Archer* v. *Woodward* [1959] Crim. L.R. 461. Also the fact that he stopped as soon as he felt the effect of the drink: *Duck* v. *Peacock* [1949] 1 All E.R. 318. The fact that unknown to him the accused suffered a liver mal-function affecting his susceptibility to alcohol was regarded as personal to the offender and hence not a special reason in *R.* v. *Jackson & Hart* [1969] 2 W.L.R. 1339.

The smallness of the excess of alcohol over the prescribed level is part of the offence and so is not a special reason: *Delaroy-Hall* v. *Tadman*; *Watson* v. *Last*; *Earl* v. *Lloyd* [1969] 2 W.L.R. 92; *Gilligan* v. *Wright* [1968] Crim. L.R. 276, though in *Earl* v. *Lloyd* it was said that the smallness of the excess might have been a good reason for not prosecuting at all.

The fact that part of a driver's excess alcohol may have been due to a previous day's drinking (a rather suspect proposition) is not a special reason: *Punshon* v. *Rose* (1968) 113 S.J. 39. There remains a discretion in the court to disqualify or not, even where special reasons have been established: *R.* v. *Agnew* (1968) 113 S.J. 58. The fact that driving ability is unimpaired cannot be a special reason on a prescribed-level charge: *Brown* v. *Dyerson*, supra; *Taylor* v. *Austin* [1969] 1 All E.R. 539. The smallness of the distance driven to remove the car from the highway may be a special reason: *James* v. *Hall* (1968) 112 S.J. 642; *MacLeod* v. *Baxter* (Edinburgh Sheriff Court, May 16, 1969); see also *R.* v. *Agnew, supra.*

In a review judgment in *R.* v. *Jackson & Hart* [1969] 2 W.L.R. 1339 it was held that an unsuspected liver defect causing alcohol to be longer retained in the blood than usual was not special reason in connection with the prescribed alcohol level offence, nor was being crippled and dependent upon an invalid carriage special reason for not disqualifying for a refusal to give a specimen of blood or urine.

(b) In regard to endorsement.

"Special reasons" for not endorsing are a question of law not of discretion: *Muir* v. *Sutherland*, 1940 J.C. 66. They seldom are applied to the more serious offences such as those involving drink and driving. The slightness of the criminality involved in the offence might be regarded as special reason: *Smith* v. *Henderson*, 1950 J.C. 48. It is unlikely that any but the most exceptional cases involving drink and driving could expect to qualify for exemption from endorsement.

Chapter 14

THE PROBLEM OF EXPERT EVIDENCE

MUCH of the evidence necessary to prove road traffic offences can be given by lay witnesses, including evidence as to the observed effects of drink. Experienced police officers can in such cases often form a reliable opinion. The question of fitness to drive, save in the grosser cases, is not a proper question for another driver to answer: *R. v. Davies* (No. 2) [1962] 1 W.L.R. 1111. The evidence of the police surgeon would normally not go beyond a description of the clinical examination, its interpretation, and a provisional opinion whether the accused was fit to be detained, and whether he could properly be proceeded against for impairment. It is undesirable that the doctor should delay that opinion until the results of laboratory tests are known, and probably improper that he should take into account the result of the breath test. The breath test is peculiar to the Road Safety Act 1967, cannot be used to prove the prescribed level offence, and is not applied by the Act to the impairment offence. Were the doctor to have regard to the result of the breath test he would be basing his opinion in part on a matter which could not competently be founded on in evidence. There is however no way of preventing the doctor from speculating that a person under arrest for the prescribed level offence must have reached that stage either through having supplied a positive breath specimen or having refused a breath test. The doctor may properly be asked at a later stage whether the results of the laboratory tests confirm his clinical opinion or not. Originally the Road Traffic Act 1962 contained references to evidence of breath specimens, but these references were removed by amendment. It is a nice question what weight could be given to evidence of a breath test performed not in connection with the procedure laid down in the Road Safety Act 1967 but simply as an item of evidence to be considered for what it was worth in an impairment prosecution. It also seems to follow that the result of a breath test showing less than a positive reading might be admissible and competent in support of a statutory defence to the offence of being in charge while the blood alcohol exceeds the prescribed level.

In some courts doctors have been asked to express their views upon the interpretation of particular blood-alcohol or urine-alcohol figures in terms of impairment. It is doubtful if many doctors are qualified by training or experience to do so, and still more doubtful whether they are equipped to give evidence in borderline cases as to the relation of physical impairment to the deterioration of driving skills. Illogically, in England doctors have been allowed to refer to conversion tables relating blood-alcohol to urine-alcohol levels although they have no personal knowledge of these matters: *R. v. Somers* [1963] 3 All E.R. 808. The statutory relation of these levels to one another in the Road Safety Act 1967, s. 7(4), now provides some expression of the ratio between them (see p. 25). In the last mentioned case, *a fortiori,* minimum destruction-rate tables for elimination of alcohol, a matter closer to the doctor's experience, were allowed to be consulted: *R. v. Somers, supra.*

EVIDENCE OF BLOOD OR URINE TESTS UNDER THE ROAD TRAFFIC ACT 1962

The Road Traffic Act 1962, s. 2, requires the court to have regard to any evidence submitted of the proportion or quantity of alcohol or of any drug contained in the body as ascertained by analysis of a blood specimen taken with consent of, or of urine provided by, the accused at any material time. It also enables the court to treat the refusal of the accused without reasonable cause to supply a blood or urine specimen after arrest for the impairment offence as supporting any evidence given for the prosecution or rebutting any evidence given for the defence, but without prejudice to the normal requirements of proof to the high standard required in criminal cases. Refusal is not a matter affecting sentence: *R. v. Godfrey* (1967), 51 Cr. App. R. 449. The degree of support or otherwise to be attributed to such a refusal lies in the discretion of the court, and has yet to be explored, though it is clear that refusal, even without reasonable cause, need not always count against the accused: *R. v. Dick-Cleland* [1965] Crim. L.R. 440. The terms of the Road Traffic Act 1962, s. 2, do not exclude the possibility that the police might be entitled to demand *both* blood and urine specimens, or to demand a second specimen of one or other, though this interpretation has not yet been tested in the courts. The incidence of the onus of disproving or establishing the reasonableness of a refusal is unclear, and the significance of the expression "material time", particularly in view of the recognised need for two urine specimens (see p. 32), ought to receive further judicial examination. The phrase as it occurs in section 1 (3) of the Road Safety Act 1967 received consideration in *Northfield* v. *Pinder* [1969] 2 W.L.R. 50, but it does not by any means follow that the same considerations apply to the wording of the earlier Act.

The analytical evidence necessary to describe the laboratory examination of blood and urine specimens can of course only be given by highly qualified scientific witnesses. Such witnesses must for the purposes of both the impairment offence and the prescribed alcohol-level offence be authorised analysts, *i.e.* they must hold a diploma or fellowship of the Royal Institute of Chemistry of Great Britain and Ireland and a certificate granted by that Institute after examination conducted in the chemistry including the microscopy of food, drugs and water, or have held appointment as a public analyst before May 27, 1957: (The Public Analysts Regulations 1957: the Public Analysts (Scotland) Regulations 1956) or be specially authorised by the Secretary of State for the purpose. (See also p. 96.)

CERTIFICATE EVIDENCE

Section 2 of the Road Traffic Act 1962 provides that the expert evidence of blood and urine-alcohol levels in the impairment offence may be given by certificate, and these provisions are applied by section 3(8) of the Road Safety Act 1967 also to the prescribed level offence. A certificate purporting to be signed by an authorised analyst and certifying the proportion of alcohol or of any drug found in a specimen identified by the certificate, and in the case of a specimen other than a blood specimen the proportion of alcohol or of that drug in the blood which corresponds to the proportion found in the specimen, is to be evidence of the matters so certified, and of the qualification of the analyst. Where no part of the specimen was given to the accused the certificate was not valid: *R.* v. *Roberts* (1964) Cr. App. R. 300. A certificate which failed to specify the blood-alcohol proportion, though it specified the urine-alcohol, was not competent evidence: *MacLeod* v. *Nicol,*

1964 J.C. 4. Where there is error in the identification of the specimen to the analyst this may be fatal if the court is not satisfied
that the correct specimen was analysed: *Douglas* v. *Wilkinson*,
1964 S.L.T. (Sh. Ct.) 68; but where they are so satisfied it need
not render the certificate incompetent: *Lawrie* v. *Stevenson*, 1968
S.L.T. 342, *Alexander* v. *Clatworthy* (1969) 113 S.J. 387. Such
a certificate is to be competent evidence for the prosecution only
where a copy has been served upon the accused at least seven
days before the date of the trial. Proof of service is therefore
required. If the accused not less than three days before the trial
has served notice on the prosecutor requiring the attendance at
the trial of the expert by whom the certificate was signed the
certificate is deprived of its special evidential value: *Herron* v.
Whitehill, 1969 S.L.T. 238. It would probably be unwise to rely
upon this notice as sufficient to bring the witness, and he should
be cited to attend in the usual way. (See also pp. 74-75.)

Where an analyst's certificate showed a very high alcohol content but the doctor conducting the clinical examination refused to
certify him as impaired and gave evidence that he did not regard
the tests as reliable, the trial judge was entitled to reject the
evidence of the certificate: *MacNeil* v. *Fletcher*, 1966 J.C. 18.

It may be observed that these provisions do not appear to
restrict the use of certificate evidence to the prosecution, and
indeed there is no such restriction in the Road Safety Act 1967 in
regard to the laboratory analysis of specimens. So far as that Act
is concerned the defence seems to be equally at liberty to submit
specimens to an authorised analyst for examination under the
Act. It is however curious that there is no provision in regard to
defence certificates corresponding to that which suspends the effect
given to prosecution certificates when the expert is called to give
evidence. It may be that this confers an immunity upon defence
certificates which the calling of the defence expert does not remove.
On the other hand this apparent omission may point rather to the
fact that the Act was not intended to place analysis facilities at
the disposal of the defence, although the specific terms of the
proviso to section 2(2) render this interpretation rather unlikely.

There has been considerable discussion in foreign countries as
to whether a person should be convicted on nothing more than
the certificate or even the oral evidence of a single analyst—*cf.
Ryan*; *Slough & Wilson*. English law permits this if the evidence
is accepted and believed, and convictions based upon nothing but

unequivocal scientific evidence are by no means unknown. Because of the general rule of Scots law that evidence however credible of the crucial facts in any criminal prosecution must be corroborated (*cf. Bisset* v. *Anderson*, 1949 J.C. 106) the prescribed alcohol-level prosecution in Scotland in which the analyst is called to give evidence may raise difficulties. There can hardly be a situation in which the evidence to convict is more crucial than in this type of case which is governed by the statutory restriction upon mode of proof. It is arguable therefore that in such a situation there must be corroboration of the accused's alcohol level, and this can only be afforded by a second analyst's evidence that he carried out a second analysis or that he independently checked the first analyst's results as he performed the analysis. There is not the same difficulty in connection with the impairment offence where other evidence usually points to the accused's ability to drive properly being impaired.

As we have explained it is not possible by modern analytical techniques to provide a precisely known figure for the alcohol in any specimen. The working figure must have certain tolerances set off to allow for error. It is common therefore (though the Act does not seem to contemplate it) to give the analytical result in a form "not less than . . . milligrammes/100 millilitres." (See p. 96.) Where this is done and it is necessary to find corroboration of the excess alcohol, the imprecise nature of the reported figure may render corroboration more difficult than if the figure were absolute. The prescribed limit, however, being a precise one, it is no defence that the excess of blood alcohol above the limit is nominal : *Gilligan* v. *Wright* [1968] Crim. L.R. 276; and this does not supply special reasons for non-disqualification : see p. 153. The *de minimis* considerations which may apply elsewhere—*cf. Briere* v. *Hailstone* [1969] Crim. L.R. 36—do not apply to this offence.

There is a further provision in section 3(9) of the Road Safety Act 1967 that in any prosecution for the impairment offence or for the prescribed alcohol-level offence a certificate purporting to be signed by a medical practitioner that he took a specimen of blood from a person with his consent shall be evidence of the matters so certified and of the qualifications of the medical practitioner. This means of avoiding the attendance of the doctor may be acceptable in the precribed level offence, but is unlikely to be acceptable in the impairment case unless the doctor was one who was unconcerned with clinical examination. The proviso also applies that such a certificate shall only be evidence where a copy was served on the accused seven days before the trial, and not if the accused serves notice at least three days before the trial upon the prosecutor requiring the doctor's attendance. The provision of section 2(3) whereby the certificate shall in proceedings in Scotland be sufficient evidence of the matters contained in the certificate applies to the doctor's certificate as it does to the analyst's.

FURTHER READING

SCIENTIFIC AND LEGAL

Chapter 1

ALEXIS LICHINE'S *Encyclopaedia of Wines and Spirits*. (Cassell & Co., London, 1967.)

Chapter 2

HARGER, R. N. & FORNEY, R. B. (1967): Chapter "Aliphatic Alcohols" in *Progress in Chemical Toxicology*, ed. A. Stolman. (Academic Press New York and London, 1967.)

JACOBSEN, E. (1952): "The Metabolism of Ethyl Alcohol," *Nature*, Vol. 169, p. 645. (Report of a lecture.)

LESTER, D. (1965): "Factors Influencing the Metabolism and Disappearance of Alcohol," *Alcohol and Traffic Safety*, p. 267. (Proceedings of the Fourth International Conference on Alcohol and Traffic Safety, 1965; Indiana University, 1966.)

PAWAN, G. L. S. (1968): "Physical Exercise and Alcohol Metabolism in Man," *Nature*, Vol. 218, p. 966.

WAYNE, E. J. (1962): "Alcohol and Driving—the Pharmacological Background," *Alcohol and Road Traffic*, p. 113. (Proceedings of Third International Conference, on Alcohol and Road Traffic, London, 1962, B.M.A., London 1963.) (A simple authoritative review.)

Chapter 3

BEGG, T. B., HILL, I. D. & NICKOLLS, L. C. (1962): A Statistically-Planned Comparison of Blood and Breath Alcohol Levels," *Alcohol and Road Traffic*, p. 277. (B.M.A., London 1963.)

BRITISH MEDICAL ASSOCIATION: *The Drinking Driver* (London 1965).

DUBOWSKI, K. M. (1962): "Unsettled Issues and Practices in Chemical Testing for Alcohol," *Alcohol and Road Traffic*, p. 203. (B.M.A., London 1963.)

FORNEY, R. B., HARGER, R. N., HUGHES & RICHARDS (1964): "Alcohol Distribution in the Vascular System," *Quarterly Journal of Studies on Alcohol*, Vol. 25, p. 205.

FROENTJES, W. (1962): "An Analysis of 10,000 Blood Tests in the Netherlands," *Alcohol and Road Traffic*, p. 179. (B.M.A., London 1963.)

HARGER, R. N. (1962): "Blood Source and Alcohol Level; Errors from using Venous Blood during Active Absorption," *Alcohol and Road Traffic*, p. 212. (B.M.A., London 1963.)

HARGER, R. N. & FORNEY, R. B. (1967): Chapter in *Progress in Chemical Toxicology*, Vol. III, ed. A. Stolman. (Academic Press, New York and London 1967.)

PAYNE, J. P., FOSTER, D. V. & HILL, D. W. & WOOD, D. G. L.: "Observations on Interpretation of Blood Alcohol Levels Derived from Analysis of Urine," *British Medical Journal*, 1967, Vol. 3, p. 819.

PAYNE, J. P., HILL, D. W. & KING, N. W.: "Observations on the Distribution of Alcohol in Blood, Breath and Urine," *British Medical Journal*, 1966, Vol. 1, p. 196.

Chapter 4

BJERVER, K. & GOLDBERG, L.: "Effect of Alcohol Ingestion on Driving Ability," *Quarterly Journal of Studies on Alcohol*, 1950, Vol. 11, p. 1.

BORKENSTEIN, R. F., CROWTHER, R. F., SHUMATE, R. P., ZIEL, W. B. & ZYLMAN, R.: *The Role of the Drinking Driver in Traffic Accidents* [Report on the Grand Rapids Survey]. (Department of Police Administration, Indiana University 1964.)

BRITISH MEDICAL ASSOCIATION (1960): *Relation of Alcohol to Road Accidents.*

COHEN, J.: "Strategic Considerations in the Study of Alcohol and Road Traffic," *Alcohol and Road Traffic*, p. 14. (B.M.A., London 1963.)

DREW, G. C., COLQUHOUN, W. P. & LONG, H. A.: *Effect of Small Doses of Alcohol on a Skill Resembling Driving.* (Medical Research Council Memorandum no. 38, H.M.S.O., London (1959.)

GOLDBERG, L. & HAVARD, J. D. J.: *Research on the Effects of Alcohol and Drugs on Driver Behaviour.* (Organisation for Economic Co-Operation and Develpoment, Paris 1968.)

HADDON, W. (Jr.): "Alcohol and Highway Accidents," *Alcohol and Road Traffic*, p. 3. (B.M.A., London 1963.)

Chapter 5

The Drinking Driver. (B.M.A., London 1965.)

The Practical Police Surgeon, Chaps. 10 and 11. (Sweet and Maxwell, London 1969.)

Chapter 6

There is a vast body of technical literature, which it would be purposeless to list here, on the analysis of body fluids for alcohol.

The following should prove useful starting points for any readers who seek further information on this subject. (All in English unless stated.)

Breath analysis

BORKENSTEIN, R. F.: "The Evolution of Modern Instruments for Breath-Alcohol Analysis," *Journal of Forensic Sciences* (1960), Vol. 5, p. 395.

BORKENSTEIN, R. F. & SMITH, H. W.: "The Breathalyzer and its Applications," *Medicine, Science and the Law*, (1961), Vol. 1, p. 13.

COLDWELL, B. B. & GRANT, G. L. (1963-I): "A Study of Some Factors Affecting the Accuracy of the Breathalyzer," *Journal of Forensic Sciences,* Vol. 8, p. 149.

SMITH, H. W. & LUCAS, D. M.: "The Development of a Large Scale Breath Testing Programme in Ontario," *Alcohol and Road Traffic*, p. 189. (B.M.A., London 1963.)

The "Alcotest" in other countries

(In Germany) GROSSKOPF, K.: "Experiences in Using the 'Alcotest' for Testing Breath as a Guide to Alcohol Concentration in the Blood," *Alcohol and Road Traffic*, p. 281. (B.M.A., London 1963.)

(In Sweden) BJERVER, K., ANDRÉASSON, R. & BONNICHSEN, R.: "A Field Study of the Use of 'Alcotest' in Sweden," *Alcohol and Traffic Safety*, p. 190. (Indiana University 1966.)

Methods of analysis of blood and urine

All of the chemical methods mentioned in this chapter, except the *Nickolls* one, are described in: NICKOLLS, L.C.; *The Scientific Investigation of Crime*, pp. 340-345. (Butterworth, London 1956.)

The *Nickolls* method is described in: NICKOLLS, L. C.: *Analyst* (1960), Vol. 85, p. 840.

A critical evaluation and comparison of both chemical and biochemical methods, with a very full bibliography, appears in: LUNDQUIST, F.: *Methods of Biochemical Analysis*, Vol. 7, p. 218. (Interscience, 1959.)

The gas-chromatographic method now generally used in this country (sometimes with slight modifications) is described in: CURRY, A. S., WALKER, G. W. & SIMPSON, G. S.: *Analyst* (1966), Vol. 91, p. 742.

A comparison of the accuracy of various methods appears in:
KRAULAND, W. & VIDIC, E.: *Blutalkhohol* (1964), Vol. 2, p. 321. (In German.)

Chapter 7

Most books dealing with the statistical evaluation of analytical results are highly technical. The following, however, are specifically addressed to the scientific layman:
M. J. MORONEY: *Facts from Figures* (Pelican Books; frequently reprinted). Easier than the following.
RUSSELL LANGLEY: *Practical Statistics for Non-Mathematical People* (Pan Books 1968). More advanced than the previous; no index.

Chapter 9

BEWLEY, T. H.: "Drugs and Driving," *The Criminologist* (1969), Vol. 4, no. 12 (May), p. 7. (Based mainly on GOLDBERG & HAVARD, *see below*.)
CARPENTER, J. A. & VARLEY, M.: *Alcohol and Road Traffic*, p. 156. (B.M.A., London 1963.)
GOLDBERG, L. & HAVARD, J. D. J.: *Research on the Effects of Alcohol and Drugs on Driving Behaviour* (O.E.C.D. Paris 1968).

Chapter 10

The Recognition of Intoxication. (B.M.A. 1954.)
Recognition of Intoxication, revised edition. (B.M.A. 1958.)
Relation of Alcohol to Road Accidents. (B.M.A. 1960.)
Alcohol and Road Traffic (Proceedings on the Third International Conference on Alcohol and Road Traffic, B.M.A. 1963.)
The Drinking Driver. (B.M.A. 1965.)
Alcohol and Traffic Safety. (Proceedings of the Fourth International Conference on Alcohol and Traffic Safety, Indiana University 1966.)
Road Safety Legislation 1965-66. (H.M.S.O. Cmnd. 2859.)
BOWDEN, K. M.: "Driving under the Influence of Alcohol" (1962) J. For. Med., Vol. 9, p. 86; (1963) Vol. 10, pp. 111 and 148; (1964) Vol. 11, p. 6; (1965) Vol. 12, p. 93; (1966) Vol. 13, p. 44.
BREITENECKER, R.: "Alcohol Testing Program in Europe" (1960) J. For. Sci., Vol. 5, p. 433.
HAGAN & OSBOROUGH, N.: "The Drinking Motorist and the Road Traffic Act (N.I.) 1964: (1967) *Northern Ireland Law Quarterly*, Vol. 18, p. 395.
LASOK, D. "The Problem of Criminal Responsibility of Drunken Drivers" (1962) Sol. Quarterly, Vol. 1, p. 47.
MURPHY, H. F.: "Chemical Tests for Intoxication: A Criticism" [1964] *New Zealand Law Journal*, pp. 491, 511.

Chapter 11

ADAMS, J. N.: "Doubts about the Breathalyzer," (1969) *Law Guardian* No. 51, p. 21.

BROWN, W. A.: "Attempt in Road Traffic Offences," 1968 S.L.T. (News.), p. 113.

BROWN, W. A.: "The Road Safety Act 1967, Pt. 1" (1967), J.L.S. Vol. 12, p. 471.

BROWN, W. A.: "The Balloon Goes Up" (1969) J.L.S. Vol. 14, p. 126.

COOPER, H. E. & BAMFORD, B. R.: *South African Motor Law*, 1965, containing Chapter 18, "Medico-Legal Aspects of Acute Alcoholic Intoxication," H. A. Shapiro.

ELLIOTT, D. W. & STREET, H.: *Road Accidents*, Penguin Books Ltd.

FITZGERALD, P. J. & POLE, K. F. M.: "The Road Safety Act 1967" (1969) New L.J., Vol. 119, pp. 43 and 61.

HAVARD, J. D. J.: "Alcohol and Road Accidents" [1962] *Practitioner*, pp. 188, 498.

HAVARD, J. D. J.: "Recent Developments in the Alcohol and Road Traffic Situation" (1963) *British Journal of Addiction*, p. 55.

HAVARD, J. D. J.: "The Road Safety Bill, Pt. 1—A Medical View" [1967] Crim. L. R., p. 151.

KEITH & CLARKE: "What is a Road?" [1959] Crim. L. R., p. 326.

LADD M. & GIBSON, R. B.: "Legal-Medical Aspects of Blood Tests to Determine Intoxication" (1943) Ann. Int. Med., Vol. 18, p. 564.

LADD M. & GIBSON, R. B.: "Medico-Legal Aspects of the Blood Test to Determine Intoxication" (1939) *Iowa Law Review*, Vol. 24, p. 191.

NEWARK, M.: "Failure to Object to an Irregularity" [1968] Crim. L. R., p. 310.

SEAGO, P.: "Offences under the Road Safety Act 1967" [1969] Crim. L. R., p. 292.

SIMPSON, Sir J.: "Police Procedure in Relation to the Drinking Driver in Alcohol and Road Traffic," p. 49. (B.M.A. 1963.)

SMITH, H. WARD: "Drinking and Driving;" (1960) *Criminal Law Quarterly*, Vol. 3, p. 65.

SMITH, J. C.: "Alcohol and Road Traffic—The English Law and its Reformation," *Alcohol and Road Traffic*, p. 299. (B.M.A. 1963.)

SMITH, J. C. & HOGAN: Criminal Law, Chap. 14. (Butterworth, 2nd ed., 1969.)

SWEENY, J.: "Sound Motion Pictures as Evidence of Intoxication" (1965) *Cornell Law Quarterly*, Vol. 52, p. 323.

WILLIAMS, GLANVILLE: "Absolute Liability in Traffic Offences" [1967] Crim. L. R., p. 194.

WRIGHT, B. M.: "Alcohol the Motorist and the Law" (1967) New L.J. Vol. 117, pp. 631 and 659.

"What is Driving?" 1949 S.L.T. (News.), p. 94.

Chapter 13

Young, N.: "Special Reasons," 1966 S.L.T. (News.), p. 113.

Chapter 14

Nokes, G. D.: "Self-Incrimination by the Accused in English Law" (1966) *University of British Columbia Law Review*, Vol. 2, p. 316.
Nokes, G. D.: "Real Evidence" (1949) *Law Quarterly Review*, Vol. 65, p. 57.
Ryan, S.: "Use of Chemical Tests to Prove Impairment by Alcohol" (1959) *Criminal Law Quarterly*, Vol. 2, p. 41.
Slough & Wilson: "Alcohol & the Motorist: Practical and Legal Problems of Chemical Testing" (1960) *Minnesota Law Review*, Vol. 44, p. 673.

APPENDIX 2

SCIENTIFIC REFERENCES

The following is a list of all the scientific references cited, *except those which have already been given in Appendix 1*. It is *not* a complete bibliography, which would be at least ten times as long.

The following contractions are used for the names of journals which appear several times in the list:

Acta pharmac. tox.: *Acta pharmacologica et toxicologica* (Copenhagen —mainly in English).

Annls. Méd. lég.: *Annales de Médicine légale, de Criminologie et de Police scientifique.*

B.M.J.: *British Medical Journal.*

Br. J. Addict.: *British Journal of Addiction to Alcohol and other Drugs.*

Dt. Z. ges. ger. Med.: *Deutsche Zeitschrift für die gesamte gerichtliche Medizin.*

J. Amer. Med. Ass.: *Journal of the American Medical Association.*

J. foren. Sci.: *Journal of Forensic Sciences* (American).

J. foren. Sci. Soc.: *Journal of the Forensic Science Society* (British).

Med. Sci. Law: *Medicine, Science and the Law.*

Q. Jl. Stud. Alc.: *Quarterly Journal of Studies on Alcohol.*

Full titles, when given, are in italics.

The following volumes are cited frequently:

Alcohol and Road Traffic: Proceedings of the Third International Conference on Alcohol and Road Traffic, London, 1962. (B.M.A., London, 1963.)

Alcohol and Traffic Safety: Proceedings of the Fourth International Conference on Alcohol and Traffic Safety, Indiana University, 1965. (Indiana University, 1966.)

H. ELBEL & F. SCHLEYER: *Blutalkohol* (Georg Thieme Verlag, Stuttgart, 1956). This is an encyclopaedic work covering the whole subject up to about 1955. In German, no English translation published. New edition in preparation but no publication date announced. Extensive bibliography. Referred to in the text of this book as *"Elbel & Schleyer."*

Note: The journal *Blutalkohol* mentioned several times in the following list (published by Verlag Deutsche Polizei, Hamburg) should not be confused with the above book of the same name; they are quite separate publications.

ABELE, G. & KROPP, R. (1958): Dt. Z. ges. ger. Med., Vol. 48, p. 68.

APEL, G. (1960): Dt. Z. ges. ger. Med., Vol. 49, p. 388.

AMERICAN MEDICAL ASSOCIATION, Committee on Problems of Motor Vehicle Accidents (1937): J. Amer. Med. Ass., Vol. 108, p. 2137.

ASTON, R. & CULLUMBINE, H. (1959): *Toxicology and Applied Pharmacology*, Vol. 1, p. 65.

BLACKMORE, D. J. (1968): J. Foren. Sci. Soc., Vol. 8, p. 73.

B.M.A. [BRITISH MEDICAL ASSOCIATION] (1953): B.M.J. (editorial note), Vol. 1, p. 1269.

B.M.A. (1967): B.M.J. (legal note), Vol. 2, p. 776.

BONNICHSEN, R. DIMBERG, R. & SJOBERG, L. (1964): *Meddelande Nr. 12 från Institutet för Maltdryckforskning* (Stockholm 1964).

BONNICHSEN, R. DIMBERG, R. MAEHLY, A. & ÅQVIST, S. (1967): *Meddelande Nr. 16 från Institutet för Maltdryckforskning* (Stockholm 1967).

BONNICHSEN, R., DIMBERG, MAEHLY & ÅQVIST (1968): *Blutalkhohol*, Vol. 5, p. 301.

BRADFORD, L. W. (1966): J. foren. Sci. Soc., Vol. 6, p. 204.

BROWN, D. J., HUGHES, F. W., FORNEY, R. B. & RICHARDS, A. B. (1965): *Alcohol and Traffic Safety*, p. 215.

BURGER, E. (1959): *Zentrallblatt für Verkehrs-Medizin*, Vol. 5, p. 23.

BUTTLE, G. A. H., FEARN, J. J. & HODGES, J. R. (1953): B.M.J., Vol. 2, p. 222.

CAMPS, F. E. & ROBINSON, A. E. (1968): Med. Sci. Law, Vol. 8, p. 153.

CASIER, H., DANECHMAND, L., SCHAEPDRYVER, A. De, HERMANS, W. & PIETTE, Y. (1966): *Arzneimittelforschung*, Vol. 16(2), p. 1505.

COHEN, J. DEARNALEY, E. J. & HANSEL, C. E. M. (1958): B.M.J., Vol. 1, pp. 1438.

COLDWELL, B B., PENNER, D. W., SMITH, H. W., LUCAS, G. H. W., RODGERS, R. F. & DARROCH, F. (1958): Q. Jl. Stud. Alc., Vol. 19, p. 590.

COLDWELL, B. B. & SMITH, H. W. (1959): *Canadian Journal of Biochemistry*, Vol. 37, p. 43.

COLDWELL, B. B. & GRANT, G. L. (1963-II): "Disappearance of Alcohol from the Blood of Diabetics," J. foren. Sci., Vol. 8, p. 220.

COLLISTER, RUBY M. (1962): *Alcohol and Road Traffic*, p. 31.

DAY, M., MUIR, G. G. & WATLING, J. (1968): *Nature*, Vol. 219, p. 1051.

DENNEMARK, H-G. (1963): *Blutalkohol*, Vol. 2, p. 166.

DITT, J. (1963): *Blutalkohol*, Vol. 2, p. 68.

DITT, J. & SCHULZE, G. (1962): *Blutalkohol*, Vol. 1, p. 183.

EEROLA, R. & ALHA, A. (1963): Dt. Z. ges. ger. Med., Vol. 53', p. 201.

ELBEL & SCHLEYER: See note at beginning of this list.

ENTICKNAP, J. B. & WRIGHT, B. M. (1965): *Alcohol and Traffic Safety*, p. 161.

ETZLER, K., JOSWIG, E. H. & MALLACH, H. J. (1968): *Archiv für Kriminologie*, Vol. 141, p. 142.

FAZEKAS, I. G. & RENGEI, B. (1969): *Blutalkohol*, Vol. 6, p. 1.

FORSTER, G., SCHULZ, G., & STARCK, H. J. (1961): *Blutalkohol*, Vol. 1, p. 2.

FOSTER, D. V. (1967): B.M.J., Vol. 1, p. 836.

FOX, B. H., HALLETT, R. A., MAKOWSKI, W., SCHNALL, A. M. & PELCH, A. (1965): *Alcohol and Traffic Safety*, p. 128.

FREUDENBERG, K. (1964): *Blutalkohol*, Vol. 2, p. 266.

GEHM, E. & SCHMID, W. (1962): Dt. Z. ges. ger. Med., Vol. 52, p. 424.

GERCHOW, J. & SACHS, V. (1961): Dt. Z. ges. ger. Med., Vol. 51, p. 32.

GOLDBERG, L. (1951): *Proceedings First International Conference Alcohol and Road Traffic* (Stockholm), p. 85.

GOLDBERG, L. (1965): *Alcohol and Traffic Safety*, p. 235.

GRÜNER, O. (1959): Dt. Z. ges. ger. Med., Vol. 49, p. 235.

HAISMAN, M. F., KIMBER, K. J. & WALLS, H. J. (1963): Br. J. Addict., Vol. 59, p. 24.

HALLERMANN, W, SACHS, V. & STEIGLEDER, E. (1960): D. Z. ges. ger. Med., Vol. 49, p. 431.

HARGER, R. N. (1965): *Alcohol and Traffic Safety*, p. 182.

HARGER, R. N., FORNEY, R. B. & BAKER, R. S. (1956): Q. Jl. Stud. Alc., Vol. 17, p. 1.

HOLCOMB, R. L. (1938): J. Amer. Med. Ass., Vol. 111, p. 1076.

ILLCHMANN-CHRIST, A. (1959): Dt. Z. ges. ger. Med., Vol. 49, p. 113.

IM OBERSTEG, J. & BÄUMLER, J. (1967): *Schweizerische Medizinische Wochenschrift*, Vol. 97, p. 1039.

JEFFCOATE, G. O. (Miss) (1958): Br. J. Addict., Vol. 55, p. 37.

JOYCE, C. R. B., EDGECOMBE, P. C. E., KENNARD, D. A. WEATHERALL, M. & WOODS, D. P. (1959): *The Journal of Mental Science*, Vol. 105, p. 51.

KAPLAN, H. L., FORNEY, R. B., RICHARDS, A. B. & HUGHES, F. W. (1965): *Alcohol and Traffic Safety*, p. 211.

KIELHOLZ, P., GOLDBERG, L., IM OBERSTEG, J., POELDINGER, W., RAMSEYER, A. & SCHMID, P. (1967): *Deutsche medizinische Wochenschrift*, Vol. 92, p. 1525.

KITAGAWA, T. (1962): *Alcohol and Road Traffic*, p. 246.

KITAGAWA, T. & WRIGHT, B. M. (1962): B.M.J., Vol. 2, p. 652.

KRAULAND, W. (1966): Dt. Z. ges. ger. Med., Vol. 57, p. 263.

KRAULAND, W., VIDIC, E., FREUDENBERG, K., SCHMIDT, B. & LENK, V. (1960): Dt. Z. ges. ger. Med., Vol. 50, p. 34.

KRAULAND, W. & VIDIC, E. (1964): *Blutalkohol*, Vol. 2, p. 321.

KRAULAND, W., MALLACH, H. J., GOSSOW, H. & FREUDENBERG, K. (1964): *Blutalkohol*, Vol. 2, p. 293.

KRAULAND, W., MALLACH, H. J., MELLEROWICZ, H. & MÜLLER, J. (1965): *Blutalkohol*, Vol. 3, p. 63.
Vol. 156, p. 432.

KULPE, W. & MALLACH, H. J. (1961): *Zeitschrift für klinische Medizin*,

LEITHOFF, H. & KOTLAREK, F. (1966): *Blutalkohol*, Vol. 3, p. 299.

LESTER, D. (1961): Q. Jl. Stud. Alc., Vol. 22, p. 554; and (1962): *ibid.*, Vol. 23, p. 17.

LINS, G. & RAUDONAT, H. W. (1962): Dt. Z. ges. ger. Med., Vol. 52, p. 242.

LOOMIS, T. A. (1962): *Alcohol and Road Traffic*, p. 119.

LOOMIS, T. A. & WEST, T. C. (1958): Q. Jl. Stud. Alc., Vol. 19, p. 30.

LUCAS, C. H. W., KALOW, W, McCOLL, J. D., GRIFFITH, B. A. & SMITH, H. W. (1953): *Proceedings Second International Conference on Alcohol and Road Traffic*, p. 139.

LUNDQUIST, F. (1961): Acta pharmac. tox., Vol. 18, p. 231.

LUNDQUIST, F. & WOLTHERS, H. (1958): Acta pharmac. tox., Vol. 14, p. 265.

McCALLUM, N. E. W. & SCROGGIE, J. G. (1963): Q. Jl. Stud. Alc., Vol. 24, p. 195.

MACHATA, G. (1967): *Blutalkohol*, Vol. 4, p. 252.

MALLACH, H. J. (1966): *Blutalkohol*, Vol. 3, p. 308.

MILLER, A. I., D'AGOSTINO, A. & MINSKY, R. (1963): Q. Jl. Stud. Alc., Vol. 24, p. 9.

MORGAN, W. H. D. (1965): J. foren. Sci. Soc., Vol. 5, p. 15.

NEWMAN, H. W., SMITH, M. E. & NEWMAN, E. J. (1959): Q. Jl. Stud. Alc., Vol. 20, p. 213.

OSTERHAUS, E. & JOHANNSMEIER, K. (1964): *Blutalkohol*, Vol. 2, p. 367.

OSTERHAUS, E. & JOHANNSMEIER, K. (1966): Dt. Z. ges. ger. Med., Vol. 57, p. 281.

OTTIS, L. (1963): *Blutalkohol*, Vol. 2, p. 25.

PAYNE, J. P., HILL, D. W. & WOOD, D. G. L. (1968): *Nature*, Vol. 217, p. 963.

PONSOLD, A. (1965): *Alcohol and Traffic Safety*, p. 127.

PONSOLD, A. & HEITE, H. J. (1960): Dt. Z. ges. ger. Med., Vol. 50, p. 228.

REES, L. (1967): Med. Sci. Law, Vol. 7, p. 26.

RENTOUL, E., SMITH, H. & BEAVERS, R. (1962): J. foren. Sci. Soc., Vol. 3, p. 2.

RAUSCHKE, J. (1968): *Blutalkohol*, Vol. 5, p. 221.

SAURY, A., BOULETREAU, P., RACHELIER-NOTTER, J. & ROCHE, L. (1966): Annls. Méd. Lég., Vol. 46, p. 179.

SCHLEYER, F. (1966): *Blutalkohol*, Vol. 3, p. 571.

SCHLEYER, F. & WICHMANN, D. (1962): *Blutalkohol*, Vol. 1, p. 234.

SCHWEITZER, H. (1968): *Blutalkohol*, Vol. 5, p. 73.

SCHWERD, W., DIMMLING, T. & KREBS, J. (1967): *Blutalkohol*, Vol. 4, p. 260.

SMITH, H. W. & POPHAM, R. E. (1951): *Proceedings of the First International Conference on Alcohol and Road Traffic* (Stockholm), p. 150.

SPRIGGS, N. I. (1958): *The Medical Press*, Vol. 240, p. 933.

STEIGLEDER, E. (1961): *Blutalkohol*, Vol. 1, p. 107.

STEVENS, P. J., MASON, J. K. & BOWDEN, C. H. (1966): Med. Sci. Law, Vol. 6, p. 96.

SUNSHINE, I., HODNETT, N., HALL, C. R. & RIEDERS, F. (1968): *Postgraduate Medicine*, Vol. 43, p. 152.

TAYLOR, J. D. & STEVENS, S. L. (1965): *Alcohol and Traffic Safety*, p. 252.

TRUHAUT, R., BOUDENE, C. & FESTY, B. (1964): Annls. Méd. Lég., Vol. 44, p. 240.

VAMOSI, M. (1958): *Soudni Lékařstvi*, Vol. 3, p. 133; 1960: *Traffic Safety*, Vol. 4(3), p. 8.

WALLS, H. J. (1958): B.M.J., Vol. 1, p. 1442; (1962): *Alcohol and Road Traffic*, p. 239.

WRIGHT, B. M. (1962): *Alcohol and Road Traffic*, p. 251.

WRIGHT, B. M. (1963): B.M.J., p. 814.

WRIGHT, B. M. (1968–I): *Nature*, Vol. 218, p. 1263; (1968–II): *Nature*, Vol. 220, p. 206.

APPENDIX 3

STATUTES

ROAD TRAFFIC ACT 1960

Driving, or being in charge, when under influence of drink or drugs

6.—(1) A person who, when driving or attempting to drive a motor vehicle on a road or other public place, is unfit to drive through drink or drugs shall be liable—

(a) on conviction on indictment, to a fine or to imprisonment for a term not exceeding two years or to both a fine and such imprisonment;

(b) on summary conviction, to a fine not exceeding one hundred pounds or to imprisonment for a term not exceeding four months or to both such fine and such imprisonment, or in the case of a second or subsequent conviction to a fine not exceeding one hundred pounds or to imprisonment for a term not exceeding six months or to both such fine and such imprisonment.

(2) [Without prejudice to the foregoing subsection, a person who, when in charge of a motor vehicle which is on a road or other public place] is unfit to drive through drink or drugs shall be liable—

(a) on conviction on indictment, to a fine or to imprisonment for a term not exceeding [twelve months] or to both a fine and such imprisonment;

(b) on summary conviction, [to a fine not exceeding one hundred pounds or to imprisonment for a term not exceeding four months] or to both such fine and such imprisonment.

A person shall be deemed for the purposes of this subsection not to have been in charge of a motor vehicle if he proves—

(i) that at the material time the circumstances were such that there was no likelihood of his driving the vehicle so long as he remained unfit to drive through drink or drugs;

(ii) [. . .].

(3) A person liable to be charged with an offence under this section

[or under section 1 or 3 of the Road Safety Act 1967] shall not be liable
to be charged—

    (*a*) under section twelve of the Licensing Act, 1872, with the offence
of being drunk while in charge, on a highway or other public place,
of a carriage, or
    (*b*) under section seventy of the Licensing (Scotland) Act, 1903,
with the offence of being drunk while in charge in a street or other
place, of a carriage—

    (4) A police constable may arrest without warrant a person commit-
ting an offence under this section.
    [(5), (6) *Repealed by the Road Traffic Act, 1962, s. 51, Sched. V,
post, Part II.*]

ROAD TRAFFIC ACT 1962

Evidence on charge of unfitness to drive

    2.—(1) In any proceedings for an offence under the said section six,
the court shall, subject to subsection (4) of this section, have regard to
any evidence which may be given of the proportion or quantity of
alcohol or of any drug which was contained in the blood or present
in the body of the accused, as ascertained by analysis [. . .] of a
specimen of blood taken from him with his consent by a medical
practitioner, or of urine [. . .] provided by him, at any material time;
and if it is proved that the accused, when so requested by a constable
at any such time, refused to consent to the taking of or to provide a
specimen for analysis [. . .], his refusal may, unless reasonable cause
therefor is shown, be treated as supporting any evidence given on
behalf of the prosecution, or as rebutting any evidence given on behalf
of the defence, with respect to his condition at that time.
    (2) For the purposes of any such proceedings, a certificate purporting
to be signed by an authorised analyst, and certifying the proportion of
alcohol or any drug found in a specimen identified by the certificate and,
in the case of a specimen not being a specimen of blood, the proportion
of alcohol or of that drug in the blood which corresponds to the proportion found in the specimen, shall be evidence of the matters so
certified and of the qualification of the analyst:
    Provided that the foregoing provision shall not apply to a certificate
tendered on behalf of the prosecution unless a copy has been served
on the accused, not less than seven days before the hearing or trial, nor
if the accused, not less than three days before the hearing or trial, or
within such further time as the court may in special circumstances allow,
has served notice on the prosecutor requiring the attendance at the
hearing or trial of the person by whom the certificate was signed.
    (3) In any such proceedings in Scotland, a certificate complying with
subsection (2) of this section and, where the person by whom such a
certificate was signed is called as a witness, the evidence of that person,
shall be sufficient evidence of the facts stated in the certificate.

(4) Where the accused, at the time a specimen of blood or urine was taken from or provided by him, asked to be supplied with such a specimen, evidence of the proportion of alcohol or any drug found in the specimen shall not be admissible on behalf of the prosecution unless—

(*a*) the specimen is either one of two taken or provided on the same occasion or is part of a single specimen which was divided into two parts at the time it was taken or provided; and

(*b*) the other specimen or part was supplied to the accused.

(5) A constable requesting any person to consent to the taking of or to provide a specimen of blood or urine for analysis shall offer to supply to him, in a suitable container, part of the specimen or, in the case of a specimen of blood which it is not practicable to divide, another specimen which he may consent to have taken.

(6) [*Repealed by the Road Safety Act 1967 (c. 30), Sched. 2, post.*]

(7) In this section "authorised analyst" means any person possessing the qualifications prescribed by regulations made under section eighty-nine of the Food and Drugs Act, 1955, or section twenty-seven of the Food and Drugs (Scotland) Act, 1956, as qualifying persons for appointment as public analysts under those Acts, and any other person authorised by the Secretary of State to make analyses for the purposes of this section.

ROAD SAFETY ACT 1967

Driving or being in charge with blood-alcohol concentration above the prescribed limit

1.—(1) If a person drives or attempts to drive a motor vehicle on a road or other public place, having consumed alcohol in such a quantity that the proportion thereof in his blood, as ascertained from a laboratory test for which he subsequently provides a specimen under section 3 of this Act, exceeds the prescribed limit at the time he provides the specimen, he shall be liable—

(*a*) on summary conviction, to a fine not exceeding £100 or to imprisonment for a term not exceeding four months or both or, in the case of a second or subsequent conviction, to a fine not exceeding £100 or to imprisonment for a term not exceeding six months or both;

(*b*) on conviction on indictment, to a fine or imprisonment for a term not exceeding two years or both.

(2) Without prejudice to the foregoing subsection, if a person is in charge of a motor vehicle on a road or other public place having consumed alcohol as aforesaid, he shall be liable—

(*a*) on summary conviction, to a fine not exceeding £100 or imprisonment for a term not exceeding four months or both;

(*b*) on conviction on indictment, to a fine or imprisonment for a term not exceeding twelve months or both.

(3) A person shall not be convicted under this section of being in charge of a motor vehicle if he proves that at the material time the circumstances were such that there was no likelihood of his driving it so long as there was any probability of his having alcohol in his blood in a proportion exceeding the prescribed limit.

(4) In determining for the purposes of the last foregoing subsection the likelihood of a person's driving a motor vehicle when he is injured or the vehicle is damaged, the jury, in the case of proceedings on indictment, may be directed to disregard, and the court in any other case may disregard, the fact that he had been injured or that the vehicle had been damaged.

(5) Section 6(2) (ii) of the principal Act (which includes as an ingredient of a defence on a prosecution of being in charge of a motor vehicle the need to prove that the accused had not driven the vehicle between becoming impaired and the material time) shall cease to have effect.

Breath tests

2.—(1) A constable in uniform may require any person driving or attempting to drive a motor vehicle on a road or other public place to provide a specimen of breath for a breath test there or nearby, if the constable has reasonable cause—

(*a*) to suspect him of having alcohol in his body; or
(*b*) to suspect him of having committed a traffic offence while the vehicle was in motion:

Provided that no requirement may be made by virtue of paragraph (*b*) of this subsection unless it is made as soon as reasonably practicable after the commission of the traffic offence.

(2) If an accident occurs owing to the presence of a motor vehicle on a road or other public place, a constable in uniform may require any person who he has reasonable cause to believe was driving or attempting to drive the vehicle at the time of the accident to provide a specimen of breath for a breath test—

(*a*) except while that person is at a hospital as a patient, either at or near the place where the requirement is made or, if the constable thinks fit, at a police station specified by the constable;
(*b*) in the said excepted case, at the hospital;

but a person shall not be required to provide such a specimen while at a hospital as a patient if the medical practitioner in immediate charge of his case is not first notified of the proposal to make the requirement or objects to the provision of a specimen on the ground that its provision or the requirement to provide it would be prejudicial to the proper care or treatment of the patient.

(3) A person who, without reasonable excuse, fails to provide a specimen of breath for a breath test under either of the two foregoing subsections shall be liable on summary conviction to a fine not exceeding £50.

(4) If it appears to a constable in consequence of a breath test carried out by him on any person under subsection (1) or (2) of this section that the device by means of which the test is carried out indicates that the proportion of alcohol in that person's blood exceeds the prescribed limit, the constable may arrest that person without warrant except while that person is at a hospital as a patient.

(5) If a person required by a constable under subsection (1) or (2) of this section to provide a specimen of breath for a breath test fails to do so and the constable has reasonable cause to suspect him of having alcohol in his body, the constable may arrest him without warrant except while he is at a hospital as a patient.

(6) The two last foregoing subsections shall not be construed as prejudicing the provisions of section 6(4) of the principal Act (arrest of persons driving or being in charge when their ability to drive properly is impaired through drink or drugs).

(7) A person arrested under this section or under the said section 6(4) shall, while at a police station, be given an opportunity to provide a specimen of breath for a breath test there.

(8) In this section "traffic offence" means an offence under any provision of the Road Traffic Acts 1960 to 1967 or of the Road Transport Lighting Act 1957.

Laboratory tests

3.—(1) A person who has been arrested under the last foregoing section or section 6(4) of the principal Act may, while at a police station, be required by a constable to provide a specimen for a laboratory test (which may be a specimen of blood or urine), if he has previously been given an opportunity to provide a specimen of breath for a breath test at that station under subsection (7) of the last foregoing section, and either—

(a) it appears to a constable in consequence of the breath test that the device by means of which the test is carried out indicates that the proportion of alcohol in his blood exceeds the prescribed limit; or

(b) when given the opportunity to provide that specimen, he fails to do so.

(2) A person while at a hospital as a patient may be required by a constable to provide at the hospital a specimen for a laboratory test—

(a) if it appears to a constable in consequence of a breath test carried out on that person under section 2(2) of this Act that the device by means of which the test is carried out indicates that the proportion of alcohol in his blood exceeds the prescribed limit; or

(b) if that person has been required, whether at the hospital or elsewhere, to provide a specimen of breath for a breath test, but fails to do so and a constable has reasonable cause to suspect him of having alcohol in his body;

but a person shall not be required to provide a specimen for a laboratory test under this subsection if the medical practitioner in immediate charge of his case is not first notified of the proposal to make the requirement or objects to the provision of a specimen on the ground that its provision, the requirement to provide it or a warning under subsection (10) of this section would be prejudicial to the proper care or treatment of the patient.

(3) A person who, without reasonable excuse, fails to provide a specimen for a laboratory test in pursuance of a requirement imposed under this section shall be guilty of an offence, and—

(a) if it is shown that at the relevant time he was driving or attempting to drive a motor vehicle on a road or other public place, he shall be liable to be proceeded against and punished as if the offence charged were an offence under section 1(1) of this Act; and

(b) in any other case, if it is shown that at that time he was in charge of a motor vehicle on a road or other public place, he shall be liable to be proceeded against and punished as if the offence charged were an offence under section (2) of this Act.

(4) In the last foregoing subsection "the relevant time" means—

(a) in relation to a person required under section 2(1) of this Act to provide a specimen of breath for a breath test, the time when he was so required;

(b) in relation to a person required under section 2(2) of this Act to provide such a specimen, the time of the accident;

(c) in relation to a person arrested under section 6(4) of the principal Act, the time of his arrest.

(5) So much of section 2(1) of the 1962 Act (evidence on charge of unfitness to drive) as relates to the provision of a specimen of breath shall cease to have effect, but save as aforesaid nothing in the foregoing provisions of this section shall affect the provisions of the said section 2(1).

(6) A person shall not be treated for the purposes of section 2(1) of the 1962 Act or subsection (3) of this section as failing to provide a specimen unless—

(a) he is first requested to provide a specimen of blood, but refuses to do so;

(b) he is then requested to provide two specimens of urine within one hour of the request, but fails to provide them within the hour or refuses at any time within the hour to provide them; and

(c) he is again requested to provide a specimen of blood, but refuses to do so.

(7) The first specimen of urine provided in pursuance of a request

under paragraph (*b*) of the last foregoing subsection shall be disregarded for the purposes of section 2 of the 1962 Act and section 1 of this Act.

(8) Subsections (2) to (7) of the said section 2 (ancillary provisions about evidence of fitness to drive) shall apply in relation to proceedings for an offence under section 1 of this Act as they apply in relation to proceedings for an offence under section 6 of the principal Act (driving or being in charge of a motor vehicle while the ability to drive properly is impaired through drink or drugs), but, in its application to proceedings for an offence under the said section 1, the said subsection (2) shall have effect as if the words from "and in the case" to "the specimen" were omitted.

(9) For the purposes of any proceedings for an offence under section 6 of the principal Act or section 1 of this Act a certificate purporting to be signed by a medical practitioner that he took a specimen of blood from a person with his consent shall be evidence of the matters so certified, and of the qualifications of the medical practitioner, and the proviso to sub-section (2) and subsection (3) of section 2 of the 1962 Act shall apply in relation to a certificate under this subsection and the medical practitioner who signed it as they apply in relation to a certificate under the said subsection (2) and the person who signed that certificate.

(10) A constable shall on requiring any person under this section to provide a specimen for a laboratory test warn him that failure to provide a specimen of blood or urine may make him liable to imprisonment, a fine and disqualification, and, if the constable fails to do so, the court before which that person is charged with an offence under section 1 of this Act or this section may direct an acquittal or dismiss the charge, as the case may require.

Detention of persons while affected by alcohol

4. Any person required to provide a specimen for a laboratory test under section 3(1) of this Act may thereafter be detained at the police station until he provides a specimen of breath for a breath test and it appears to a constable that the device by means of which the test is carried out indicates that the proportion of alcohol in that person's blood does not exceed the prescribed limit.

Consequences of conviction of certain offences of driving or being in charge

5.—(1) A person convicted of any of the following offences, that is to say, an offence under section 6(1) of the principal Act (driving a vehicle while the ability to drive properly is impaired), an offence under section 1(1) of this Act and an offence under section 3(3) of this Act which is punishable by virtue of paragraph (*a*) of the said sub-section (3), shall be treated for the purposes of determining his liability to punishment on a subsequent conviction of any other of those offences as having been convicted of that other offence.

(2) For the purposes of sections 5 and 7 of the 1962 Act (disqualification for holding a licence and endorsement of licences)—

(*a*) an offence under section 1(1) of this Act or an offence under section 3(3) of this Act which is punishable by virtue of paragraph (*a*) of the said subsection (3) shall be treated as if it were an offence under section 6(1) of the principal Act and accordingly as if it were an offence specified in Part I of Schedule 1 to the 1962 Act (offences involving obligatory disqualification); and

(*b*) any other offence under the said section 1 or 3 shall be treated as if it were an offence under section 6(2) of the principal Act and accordingly as if it were an offence specified in Part II of the said Schedule 1 (offences involving discretionary disqualification).

Application of Part I to the Crown
6.—(1) This Part of this Act shall apply to vehicles and persons in the public service of the Crown and shall, in its application to persons subject to service discipline, apply outside as well as within Great Britain and have effect as if—

(*a*) references to a constable included references to a member of the provost staff;

(*b*) references to a hospital included references to a naval, military or air force unit or establishment at which medical or surgical treatment is provided for persons subject to service discipline;   ..

(*c*) references to a police station included references to a naval, military or air force unit or establishment;

(*d*) references to proceedings for an offence under any enactment included references to proceedings for the corresponding service offence;

(*e*) references to the court included a reference to any naval, military or air force authority;

(*f*) in section 2(1) the reference to a traffic offence included a reference to the corresponding service offence; and

(*g*) in section 3(10) the reference to disqualification were omitted and for the reference to directing an acquittal there were substituted a reference to finding the person not guilty without further proceeding with the case.

(2) In relation to persons for the time being subject to service discipline the power of arrest conferred on a constable by section 6(4) of the principal Act (arrest of persons driving or being in charge when their ability to drive properly is impaired) shall also be exercisable by a member of the provost staff and shall be so exercisable outside as well as within Great Britain.

(3) In this section—

"Corresponding service offence," in relation to an offence under any enactment, means an offence under section 42 of the Naval Discipline Act 1957 or an offence against section 70 of the Army Act 1955 or section 70 of the Air Force Act 1955, committed by an act or omission which is punishable under that enactment or would be so punishable if committed in Great Britain;

"member of the provost staff" means a provost officer or any person legally exercising authority under or on behalf of a provost officer;

"persons subject to service discipline" means persons subject to the said Act of 1957, to military law or to air force law and other persons to whom section 42 of the said Act of 1957 or section 70 of either of the said Acts of 1955 for the time being applies; and

"provost officer" means a person who is a provost officer within the meaning of the said Act of 1957 or either of the said Acts of 1955.

Interpretation of Part I

7.—(1) In this Part of this Act, except so far as the context otherwise requires—

"breath test" means a test for the purpose of obtaining an indication of the proportion of alcohol in a person's blood carried out, by means of a device of a type approved for the purpose of such a test by the Secretary of State, on a specimen of breath provided by that person;

"disqualification" means disqualification for holding or obtaining a licence to drive a motor vehicle granted under Part II of the principal Act;

"fail", in relation to providing a specimen, includes refuse and "failure" shall be construed accordingly;

"hospital" means an institution which provides medical or surgical treatment for in-patients or out-patients;

"laboratory test" means the analysis of a specimen provided for the purpose.

"the prescribed limit" means 80 milligrammes of alcohol in 100 millilitres of blood or such other proportion as may be prescribed by regulations made by statutory instrument by the Minister.

(2) A person shall be treated for the purposes of this Part of this Act as providing a specimen of blood if, but only if, he consents to the specimen being taken by a medical practitioner and it is so taken and shall be treated for those purposes as providing it at the time it is so taken.

(3) References in this Part of this Act to providing a specimen of breath for a breath test are references to providing a specimen thereof in sufficient quantity to enable that test to be carried out.

(4) For the purposes of this Part of this Act 107 milligrammes of alcohol in 100 millilitres of urine shall be treated as equivalent to 80 milligrammes of alcohol in 100 millilitres of blood, and the power conferred by subsection (1) of this section to prescribe some other proportion of alcohol in the blood shall include power to prescibe a proportion of alcohol in urine which is to be treated as equivalent to the prescribed proportion of alcohol in the blood.

(5) The Minister shall not make any regulations under subsection (1) of this section unless a draft of the regulations has been approved by both Houses of Parliament.

Arrest without warrant of persons driving while disqualified

30.—A constable in uniform may arrest without warrant any person driving or attempting to drive a motor vehicle on a road whom he has reasonable cause to suspect of being disqualified for holding or obtaining a licence granted under Part II of the principal Act.

INDEX

A

Accident,
  breath test if suspected, 132, 134, 135
  definition, 135
  effect of blood-alcohol concentration on, 52-61, 114
  probability of, 58, 61
Accuracy,
  analysis, of, 89-96
  definition of, 90
Addicts and driving, 106
ADH, 17
  analysis by, 80, 81, 88
Alcohol,
  absolute, 3, 5
  absorption of, 8-9, 14-16
  blood, in: *see* Blood alcohol
  breath, in, 34-37
  "consumed," 117
  effects of: *see* Blood alcohol, effect of
  endogenous, 20
  ethyl, 1
  see also Ethanol
  habituation to, 43
  having "consumed", 131
  level,
    detention until dropped, 125
    see also Blood alcohol, concentration
  mouth, in, effect of on breath alcohol, 37
  reasonable cause to suspect, 132
  solutions of,
    percentage, definition, 3
    specific gravities of, 3-4
Alcohol dehydrogenase: *see* ADH
Alcoholics, 18, 39, 43
Alcohols, definition and nomenclature, 1-2
Alcotest, 78-79, 138-139

approval of, 136, 139-140
best evidence rule, 139
borderline readings on, 138
colour change in, significance of, 138
defective, 137, 139
destruction of, 139
deterioration of, 139
failure of, 136
incompetent as to alcohol level, 135
interpretation of,
  constable, by, 138
production of as exhibit, 138
Alkohol Minus (ALMI), 22
Alternative charges, 123
American Medical Association, 45
Amphetamine and derivatives: *see* stimulants
Analgesics, 103
Analysis,
  accuracy of, 89-96
  automatic, 88
  blood and urine, 79-88
    biochemical methods for, 81
    chemical methods for, 80-81
    criteria for, 79
    physical methods for, 82
    use made of, 117
  breath, 76-79
  gas chomatography, by, 82-87, 95-98
  mistakes in, allegations of, 97-98
  precautions in, 74, 97-98
Analysts, authorised, 96, 157
Anti-depressants, 104
Anti-histamines, 104
Arrest, 126, 146
  after interval,
    impairment offence, for, 148
  bail, right to, 126
  breath test, after,
    if negative, 148

* Only the chemically specific references to ethanol are given here. Most
of the entries relating to it will be found under "Alcohol."

M

Mandatory testing, 115
Material time,
defence to in-charge offence, 123
doctor's evidence of, 128
in charge, 122
laboratory specimens, 140, 156
urine specimens, 157
Mechanical dumpers, 119
Medical examination: see Clinical examination
Motor vehicle,
defective, 120
definition, 119
earth scraper, 119
Go-kart, 119
mechanical dumper, 119
powered lawn mower, 120
road roller, 120
Moving-traffic offence, 132
breath test as soon as possible after, 138
Muscular activity, effect of on blood-alcohol curve, 19

N

n-propanol: see under Propanol
Nickolls method of analysis, 81
Nystagmus, 41, 110, 130

O

Objections to evidence, 130
Offences abroad, 118
Opportunity to provide further breath test, 36, 140

P

Pedal cycles, 115
Penalties, 149-154, App. 3
breath specimen, failure to provide, 150
impairment offence, 149
in-charge offences, 150
laboratory specimen, failure to provide, 151
prescribed-level offence, 149
special reasons for not disqualifying, 152
special reasons for not endorsing licence, 154
Police,
failure to caution and charge, 147
evidence of driver's conduct, 126
instructions for breath test, 136

intention to prosecute, 148
obligatory acts of,
breath test demand, 136
offer of specimen to accused, 142
uniform to be worn for breath test, 133
powers,
none to demand second breath test, 137
to detain, 124
to stop vehicle, 134
procedure in impairment offence, 147
reason to suspect unfitness, 126, 132
station, clinical examination at, 127
Police Surgeons, Association of, of Great Britain, 64
Potable liquors: see Liquors, potable
Powered lawn mower, 120
Precision, definition of, 90
Prejudice,
delay in offering blood specimen, 141
failure to give warning, 140
patient in hospital, 135, 141
Prescribed level, 118, 130, App. 3
Prescribed level offence,
additional drink consumed, 128
advocated, 115
arrest necessary, 147
attempts, 122
breath test not evidence, 135
constable to read Alcotest, 138
crown servants, application to, 118
definition, 130
detention under, 124
drugs not involved with, 131
effect of non co-operation, 132
evidence by certificate, 157
impairment, no need to prove, 132, 153
in charge, 123
introduced, 117
penalties, 149, App. 3
procedure must be correct at each stage, 131
proved by laboratory tests only, 140
servicemen, application to, 118
smallness of excess, 153, 159
social justification for, 45, 132